RENTING AN

This book describes the legal implications
of renting or letting a home
in the private or public sector
in England and Wales.
It does not apply in Scotland
and Northern Ireland.

a Consumer Publication

text provided by   Ruth Annand and Jonathan Hill
University of Bristol

edited by   Edith Rudinger

published by   Consumers' Association
publishers of **Which?**

Which? Books are commissioned and researched
by The Association for Consumer Research
and published by Consumers' Association,
2 Marylebone Road, London NW1 4DX and
Hodder and Stoughton, 47 Bedford Square,
London WC1B 3DF

© Consumers' Association Ltd
May 1989

ISBN 0 85202 395 2
and 0 340 48606 6

Photoset by Paston Press, Loddon, Norfolk
Printed in Great Britain by
Galliard (Printers) Ltd, Great Yarmouth

RENTING and LETTING

a Consumer Publication

Consumers' Association
publishers of **Which?**
2 Marylebone Road
London NW1 4DX

CONTENTS

Throughout this book

for 'he' read 'he or she'

A BRIEF OUTLINE OF THE RELEVANT LAW

It is important to be aware of the general principles which are relevant in the context of the relationship between landlord and tenant. The law in this area is very complex and the use of some technical vocabulary cannot be avoided altogether.

The first part of this chapter (freehold and leasehold interests) sets out the relevant common law. The common law has been developed over the centuries, primarily by the courts rather than by Parliament.

The common law – although underpinning the whole system – is today only a small part of the law governing the relationship between landlords and tenants. During the course of this century, the common law has been to a great extent overtaken by legislative schemes which regulate the rights and duties of landlords and tenants in considerable detail. The basic outline of these schemes is discussed in the second part of this chapter (statutory schemes of protection).

freehold and leasehold interests

In English law, the two types of interest in land which are capable of being legal estates are freehold and leasehold. A legal estate confers on the owner rights which are enforceable against the whole world and, as such, legal estates form the basis of conveyancing transactions. 'Land' includes houses or flats or other property standing on the land.

A freehold interest is the equivalent of absolute ownership of land. A freehold interest is characterised by the fact that it is capable of lasting for ever. The owner may sell it, or make a gift of it (either by will or during his lifetime). If the owner does not expressly leave the interest to someone on his death, the interest will pass to relatives under intestacy rules. Leasehold differs from freehold in two important respects. First, a lease-hold interest is, in principle, of a fixed duration: it arises where a person is granted a right to occupy land for a specified period (such as a month, a year, or a number of years). Secondly, the creation of a leasehold interest gives rise to rights and obli-gations between the person granting it and the person to whom the interest is granted.

Normally the right to occupy land is granted in return for the payment of a sum of money (which in the context of the leasehold relationship is called rent).

Most agreements creating leasehold interests also contain other terms setting out the rights and duties of the parties, for example, as to the carrying out of repairs, and the tenant's use of the property. These terms are known as express covenants. In addition, even if the agreement does not expressly create obligations, the law will imply certain obligations between the parties, which are called implied covenants.

A leasehold interest is called a lease or a tenancy, and these terms tend to be used interchangeably. The word 'lease' is also used to describe the document which confers on the occupier the right to occupy and enjoy the premises in question. However, a tenancy can arise in certain circumstances as a result of an oral (or even implied) agreement without there being any formal documentation.

The person who occupies land on the basis of a leasehold interest is referred to as a tenant (or lessee), and the person who has granted the lease is known as the landlord (or lessor). Where land is occupied by a tenant, the landlord will normally be the owner of the freehold interest. The landlord's interest is known as a reversion because when the lease expires, the property reverts to the landlord.

A tenant may grant the right to occupy and enjoy the land to another person. This arrangement is called a sub-tenancy or a sub-lease, and the new occupier is known as a sub-tenant (or sub-lessee). A sub-lease must be for a period which is shorter than the leasehold out of which it is created, and a hierarchy of interests may be created. In such a situation, the owner of the freehold interest is known as the head-landlord, and the parties between the freeholder and the actual occupier of the premises are known as intermediate landlords. An intermediate landlord is both a tenant (of his landlord) and a landlord (of his tenant).

A tenancy is often regarded as inferior to a freehold interest, because it is an interest of limited duration. However, legislation has introduced a variety of schemes of protection which confer on certain categories of tenant a number of important rights. First, legislation gives security of tenure to many tenants. Security of tenure allows the tenant to remain in occupation for longer than the period envisaged by the terms of the lease itself. Secondly, legislation has given certain categories of tenant the right to buy. The right to buy entitles tenants in certain circumstances to purchase the landlord's interest.

A tenancy – even if granted for a short duration – is in economic and human terms an asset of considerable value to the tenant.

sharing

In cases involving the sharing of residential accommodation, especially where not all the occupiers' names appear on the lease, or where each of the occupiers enters a separate agreement with the owner, or where the agreement is oral, there are a number of possibilities:

- the occupiers are joint tenants
- each occupier is a tenant of part of the premises
- one occupier is a tenant of the premises and the other occupiers are each sub-tenants of part of the premises

o the occupiers are licensees (The difference between a lease and licence is extremely important. This issue is discussed at pages 23 to 32.)

joint tenancies

While it is common for a lease to be granted to a single individual, this is not always the case. A joint tenancy exists where a lease is granted to two or more people. As far as the landlord and the rest of the world are concerned, the position of joint tenants is the same as a sole tenant. Each and every joint tenant is responsible for paying the rent and observing the covenants in the lease. (If one joint tenant pays the whole rent, he can recover from the other joint tenants their share of it.) Between themselves, the joint tenants are all equal, and no one joint tenant can exclude another from the premises.

The distinguishing feature of a joint tenancy is that if one of the joint tenants dies, his interest automatically passes to the remaining joint tenants, until there is only one survivor left. A joint tenant cannot dispose of his interest in a will. So, in a situation where husband and wife, or two friends, are joint tenants of a flat, when one dies, the other immediately becomes the sole tenant. The survivor would become the sole tenant even if the deceased had purported in his will to leave his share of the tenancy to someone else.

fixed term and periodic tenancies

A lease may be created for any period of fixed duration. It is possible to create a lease for a week, a month, a year, or a number of years. Where a developer converts a building into a number of self-contained flats, it is usual for the purchasers of the flats to be granted a long lease for say 99 years or even for 999 years in return for the payment of a capital sum. The occupier of a flat who holds a lease for 999 years is in a position very similar to that of a freeholder.

Not all fixed term tenancies are for such long periods. It is not uncommon for private landlords to grant fixed term tenancies for periods ranging between 6 months and 5 years.

A periodic tenancy is granted for a short period (month, week, year) in the first place, and then continues for further periods of that length until ended by either the landlord or the tenant.

formalities

The creation and transfer of legal estates in land requires the use of certain formalities. For example, the transfer of some types of interest must be made by deed. A deed is a formal written document which must be 'signed as a deed, witnessed and delivered'.

Fixed term tenancies tend to be created formally (that is, in writing or by deed). However, an owner of residential premises may allow a person to go into possession of the premises without having reached a formal agreement (or the formal agreement entered into by the parties may be ineffective because of some lack of formality). In such a case, the law will presume that the person who then occupies the premises, and who pays rent periodically, has a periodic tenancy. The period is determined by reference to the payment of rent: if the tenant pays rent monthly, he has a monthly tenancy; if he pays rent yearly he has a yearly tenancy.

leases for a fixed term exceeding three years
The requirement of a deed applies to leases of more than three years' duration. However, a lease for more than three years which is made in writing, or is the subject of an oral agreement and so lacks formality (that is to say, has not been created in the proper manner) may nevertheless be enforceable against the landlord as an 'agreement for a lease'.

A lease created by deed is a legal lease. An 'agreement for a lease' (which includes both a lease which lacks formality and an agreement to grant a lease at some point in the future) does not create a legal interest.

The courts regard an agreement for a lease as sufficient to create a relationship of landlord and tenant between the parties if two conditions are satisfied. First, either the agreement must have been created in writing, or – if it was oral – the tenant must have gone into possession of the premises and started paying rent. (A change in the law is, however, expected soon under which an oral agreement for a lease for over 3 years will be invalid.) Secondly, the tenant must not have acted inequitably or unfairly. If these conditions are satisfied, the courts will regard the tenant as occupying the premises under an equitable lease.

There are historical reasons for describing an agreement for a lease, or a lease which lacks formality, as an equitable lease. Until the reforms of the late nineteenth century, an agreement for a lease was only enforceable in the Court of Equity, a special court which administered a particular body of rules ('equity') separate from the common law. Today, common law and equity are administered by the same courts.

The respective rights and obligations of the landlord and the tenant will be the same regardless of whether the lease is legal or equitable. The significance of the distinction lies in the effect which they may have on third parties.

legal leases and third parties
The basic rule as regards legal leases is that legal interests 'bind the whole world'. Therefore, a person who purchases the landlord's freehold reversion will be bound by the rights of any tenant occupying the premises under a legal lease. For example: in 1987 L grants a five year lease to T, by deed. In 1989 L sells his freehold interest to A. A is bound by T's lease (which still has three years to run).

equitable leases
With regard to equitable leases, on the other hand, the position

of the tenant – in the situation of his landlord selling the freehold interest – is more precarious. Where the land is 'unregistered' the lease has to be protected by being registered as an estate contract (which is a type of land charge) against the name of the owner of the freehold estate. An equitable lease which is not registered as a land charge will not bind a purchaser of the landlord's freehold interest. The Land Charges Department in Plymouth (telephone Plymouth 779831) will tell you how to register an estate contract.

Alternatively, where the title to the property is 'registered' an equitable lease may be protected by the entry of a caution or a notice against the landlord's title. The central Land Registry in London which deals with registered land, (telephone 01-405-3488) will tell you how to lodge a caution or a notice. If an equitable lease in registered land is protected by a notice or a caution, a purchaser of the landlord's freehold interest will take the lease subject to the tenant's rights.

In registered land, even if the tenant fails to protect his interest, a purchaser of the landlord's freehold reversion will normally be bound by the tenant's interest. An equitable tenant who is in occupation of the premises at the time of the sale of the reversion will have what is known as an 'overriding interest.' The purchaser will not be able to get rid of the tenant unless, before the sale took place, the purchaser made enquiries of the tenant and the tenant failed to disclose his interest.

leases for three years or less
While a lease for more than three years, if it is to take effect as a legal lease, must be created by deed, a lease for a term of three years or less (which includes a periodic tenancy) may be created orally, or in writing. Accordingly, a periodic tenancy which arises by virtue of the tenant going into possession of a flat or house and paying rent on a weekly basis to the landlord is a legal lease.

Notwithstanding the fact that the validity of short leases and periodic tenancies does not depend on any particular formalities being satisfied, it is sensible to create these arrangements in writing, rather than orally. If the lease is in writing, the scope for argument between the landlord and the tenant on a number of points is significantly reduced.

ending a tenancy at common law

A fixed term tenancy confers on the tenant a right to occupy premises for a limited period of time. When the period of the tenancy has expired, the tenant's right under the tenancy to remain in occupation of the premises comes to an end, and the landlord is entitled to recover possession.

However, a tenancy may be brought to an end by the parties before the date on which it is due to expire, through notice to determine, surrender or forfeiture.

notice to determine

A lease for a fixed term may contain a provision whereby the tenant or the landlord (or both) is given the power to bring the tenancy to an end before the end of the fixed period on the happening of some specified event. Such a provision is known as a 'break clause'. For example, a tenancy for twenty-one years may provide for the landlord or the tenant to bring the lease to an end after seven or fourteen years. Although a break clause may be included in a tenancy for the benefit of either party, the power to give notice to determine will be exercisable only by the tenant unless the clause expressly states that the power may be exercised by the landlord.

To exercise a power to determine, the party wishing to end the tenancy serves a notice to determine (sometimes referred to as a notice to quit) on the other party in the form prescribed by the terms of the lease. Normally, the notice will have to be served within a certain time, such as six months, before the break clause date. At common law, the tenancy will come to an end on the expiry of the notice period (that is, on the break clause date), even if the other party wants the arrangement to continue.

In general, break clauses are drafted in such a way that the power to determine may be exercised at specified times, but without reasons having to be given. So, where a power to determine coincides with a rent review, the tenant may choose to bring the lease to an end if he feels that the new rent is likely to be more than he will be able to afford. Similarly, a long lease may include a break clause (giving the landlord a power to determine at five year intervals, for example) so that if redevelopment of the site becomes financially attractive during the contractual term, the landlord can opt to end the tenancy.

surrender

A tenancy may be brought to an end by the tenant surrendering his interest, that is giving up his lease, to the landlord. If the landlord accepts the surrender, the lease is extinguished. The landlord is not required to agree to a surrender and, if he refuses, the tenancy will continue and the tenant will continue to be bound by the terms of the lease.

forfeiture

All well drafted fixed term tenancies include a forfeiture clause, which entitles the landlord to bring the tenancy to an end (before the expiry of the fixed term) if the tenant is in breach of his obligations under the lease. The landlord's right to forfeit the tenancy is important since it encourages the tenant to comply with his obligations.

The normal way of forfeiting a lease is by the landlord serving a writ or summons for possession on the tenant. Alternatively, the landlord may enforce his right to forfeiture by 're-entering the land' (thereby recovering possession). It is extremely unwise for a landlord to attempt physically to re-enter residential premises, since he will expose himself to the risk of criminal prosecution.

A number of conditions have to be satisfied before the right to forfeit arises. Except where forfeiture is sought for non-payment of rent, the landlord must serve a notice on the tenant (under section 146 of the Law of Property Act 1925). The notice must

○ specify the breach complained of
○ require the breach to be remedied (if possible)
○ require the tenant to compensate the landlord for any loss.

Where a breach is capable of remedy, the landlord must give a reasonable period for the tenant to comply with the notice. Only if the tenant fails to remedy the breach may the landlord proceed to forfeit the lease.

However, while the landlord is proceeding – that is until the landlord physically recovers possession or obtains a court order for possession – the tenant may apply to the court for relief against forfeiture. The court will grant relief where it is just and equitable to do so, and on such terms as it thinks fit.

In relation to forfeiture for non-payment of rent, the landlord does not have to serve a section 146 notice. The landlord must, however, make a formal demand for the rent arrears, or be exempted from having to do so by the terms of the lease (which is usual). The tenant may apply to the court for relief against forfeiture either while the landlord is proceeding or within six months of the landlord recovering possession. While it is usual for the court to grant relief to the tenant if he pays off the rent arrears and pays the landlord's expenses, where the tenant applies to the court after the landlord has retaken possession, relief will normally not be granted if the landlord has since re-let the premises.

Although it is the service of the writ, or summons for possession, on the tenant which brings the lease to an end, in order to recover possession of the premises the landlord should obtain an order for possession from the court. The order of the court both establishes that the forfeiture is justified, and that the tenant is not entitled to relief. If, however, the court grants relief to the tenant, the effect is as if the lease had never been forfeited.

ending a periodic tenancy

Unlike a fixed term tenancy, a periodic tenancy does not come to an end by time having run out. A periodic tenancy will continue indefinitely unless the parties take steps to end it. A landlord and tenant may by agreement terminate the tenancy at any time.

The most common way in which a periodic tenancy is brought to an end is by notice to quit. At common law, either party may serve a notice to quit on the other. In relation to a yearly tenancy, a notice period of six months is required; for a quarterly tenancy, one quarter's notice; for monthly and weekly tenancies, four weeks' notice. The notice must expire on the last day of a completed period of the tenancy. At the end of the notice period, as long as the notice is effective, the tenancy comes to an end.

A notice to quit is a unilateral way of bringing a tenancy to an end; there is no requirement that the other party consents.

Where premises are occupied by joint tenants, the service of a notice to quit by one of the joint tenants will be effective to bring the tenancy to an end. The fact that the other joint tenants do not want the tenancy to be terminated is ineffective to preserve the tenancy. Similarly, the service of notice to quit by the landlord on one of a number of joint tenants will bring the tenancy to an end at common law.

Although the landlord has a right to possession as soon as the tenancy is properly brought to an end, it is not lawful (except in relation to excluded tenancies) for a landlord to enforce his right to possession otherwise than by court proceedings. If, after the expiry of a notice to quit validly served by the landlord, the tenant refuses to leave the premises, the landlord should commence proceedings with a view to obtaining an order for possession from the court.

limits of the common law

While the common law is applicable in various situations, most tenancies of residential premises are subject to statutory schemes of protection, that is, the rules under the various relevant Acts of Parliament. In relation to statutorily protected tenancies, the landlord can only recover possession according to the terms of the relevant statutory scheme.

statutory schemes of protection

In periods of housing shortage, the superior bargaining power of landlords may result in the exploitation of tenants – both in terms of increases in rent and the threat of eviction. As a response to this, Parliament introduced legislation aimed at giving tenants a number of rights against their landlord. Historically, the two most important rights were rent control and security of tenure.

Security of tenure entitles a tenant to remain in occupation unless and until the landlord can establish one of the grounds of repossession set out in the relevant legislation. As a result of security of tenure, the various ways in which tenancies may come to an end at common law (as described in the last few pages) have become significantly less important.

From the landlord's point of view, controlled rents and security of tenure are undesirable, since they can reduce the capital value of the property by as much as two-thirds. As a result, the amount of property available for renting in the private sector has declined. Also, many landlords have sought to escape from the effects of the legislation.

recent changes

In recent years, there have been a number of major shifts in housing legislation.

First, in relation to newly created tenancies in the private sector, rent control has been effectively abolished. The ostensible reason for the abolition of rent control is a desire by the government to encourage landowners in the private sector back into the renting market.

Secondly, legislation (the Leasehold Reform Act 1967) has given certain categories of tenant in the private sector the right to buy the freehold or a long lease from the landlord at a very favourable price.

Thirdly, a similar right to buy has been given to public sector tenants (such as tenants of council housing). In this way, many tenants are becoming owner-occupiers. The public sector right to buy was introduced by the Housing Act 1980 and is now contained in the Housing Act 1985.

Fourthly, recent legislation (Housing and Planning Act 1986 and Housing Act 1988) has introduced schemes whereby private entrepreneurs or organisations may purchase the housing stock from local authority landlords. Before this can take place, the occupying tenants must vote on the question as to whether they want the premises to be sold. If sale of the housing stock into the private sector does take place, the tenants will effectively be swapping their landlords – from public sector to private sector. However, the tenant's right to buy is preserved.

the different schemes

There are numerous schemes of statutory protection, each one being governed by separate legislation. Although there are certain similarities between the different schemes, the respective rights and duties of landlords and tenants depend on the technicalities of the relevant legislation, as interpreted by the courts.

Each of the statutory schemes lays down certain conditions which a tenancy has to satisfy if the tenant is to qualify for protection. Some tenancies will not be within the ambit of any statutory scheme of protection. Tenancies which do not qualify for protection are governed by the common law.

The first distinction to be drawn is between private sector tenancies, public sector tenancies and tenancies granted by housing associations and analogous bodies. A tenancy is in the public sector if the landlord is a public authority (which includes, for example, local authorities and urban development corporations). Tenancies granted by individuals, companies and other bodies which are not classified as public authorities are in the private sector. Housing associations and similar organisations share characteristics of both public and private bodies.

in the private sector

In the private sector, one of the most important factors is the date on which the tenancy in question was created.

tenancies granted on or after 15 January 1989
A tenancy granted on or after 15 January 1989 is an **assured tenancy** which is governed by the Housing Act 1988.

However, the Housing Act 1988 also enables a landlord to grant an **assured shorthold tenancy** (which must be for a fixed duration of at least six months). To create an assured shorthold, the landlord must serve an appropriate notice before the commencement of the tenancy.

tenancies granted before 15 January 1989
As a general rule, a tenancy created before 15 January 1989 is a **protected tenancy**, which is governed by the Rent Act 1977. There are, however, a number of exceptions:

○ Since 1980 there has been a category of **protected shorthold**

tenancies. In order for a tenancy to be a protected shorthold it must be for a fixed term of between one and five years, and the landlord should have served the necessary notice on the tenant before the tenancy commenced.

o A tenancy which is not a protected tenancy may be a **restricted contract** if the tenant pays for furniture or services (or if the landlord is also resident in the building which is occupied by the tenant). Restricted contracts are subject to rent control, but the tenant has no security of tenure.

o Since 1980, certain approved landlords were entitled to grant **assured tenancies** regulated by the Housing Act 1980. However, assured tenancies created before 15 January 1989 are now assured tenancies within the terms of the Housing Act 1988.

in the public sector

Tenancies granted by public authorities are **secure tenancies** governed by the Housing Act 1985 (as amended).

tenancies granted by housing associations and analogous bodies

Housing associations, housing trusts and the Housing Corporation are quasi-public bodies; not quite like local authorities nor private companies. The law prior to 15 January 1989 reflected this hybrid nature.

tenancies granted before 15 January 1989
Tenancies granted before 15 January 1989 by the Housing Corporation, housing trusts and many housing associations are **secure tenancies** under the Housing Act 1985. However, tenancies granted by housing associations which are not secure tenancies may be **protected tenancies** within the Rent Act 1977. Furthermore, since 1980, if approved by the Secretary

of State, housing associations could grant **assured tenancies** under the Housing Act 1980, and these are now assured tenancies under the Housing Act 1988.

The Rent Act 1977 introduced the notion of a **housing association tenancy.** This is a tenancy granted by a housing association, a housing trust or the Housing Corporation which is not a protected tenancy. Part IV of the 1977 Act provided for rent control in relation to housing association tenancies.

A tenancy granted by a housing association, a housing trust or the Housing Corporation before 15 January 1989 can be both a secure tenancy and a housing association tenancy.

tenancies granted on or after 15 January 1989
The Housing Act 1988 has brought new lettings by quasi-public bodies into the private sector scheme.

After 14 January 1989 tenancies granted by housing associations (other than fully mutual housing associations), housing trusts and the Housing Corporation are **assured tenancies** or **assured shorthold tenancies** under the Housing Act 1988.

avoiding the scope of statutory schemes of protection

In the public sector, avoidance of the legislation is not an issue.

In recent years, private sector landlords have seemed to show themselves to be unwilling to submit to the schemes of protection by which Parliament intended to regulate tenanted premises. A number of mechanisms for avoiding the Rent Act 1977 have been devised including making use of the distinction between leases and licences, and many of these mechanisms are still relevant in the context of the Housing Act 1988.

leases and licences

Granting a lease is not the only way in which an owner of land can profit from letting someone occupy his property. If he simply permits someone to occupy the property, this will mean that the occupier is not a trespasser or squatter. It may be agreed that the permission to occupy the premises should last for a certain length of time and that the occupier should pay a sum of money (similar to rent) for the occupation. The parties may agree other express terms – about the provision of furniture, breakages, damage, cleaning and the like. Such an arrangement, if genuine, is known as a licence. The owner is called the licensor and the occupier is the licensee. A guest staying in a hotel is a licensee.

what is a licence?

There are no formal requirements for the creation of a licence, but it is usual and preferable for a licence agreement to set out in writing the terms of the occupation.

In principle, a licence is a personal arrangement between the licensor and the licensee. It usually forms part of a contract, and can therefore be terminated only in accordance with the terms of the contract. But a contractual licensee (unlike a tenant) has no proprietary interest in the land which he occupies (this is to say, he has no stake in the property). So, a contractual licence (unlike a tenancy) cannot bind a third party: if a new landlord buys the freehold reversion, he has the right to evict the licensee, even if he knew of the existence of the licence at the time of acquisition. The only remedy available to the licensee is to sue the original licensor for damages (i.e. monetary compensation) for breach of contract.

why create a licence?

As far as landlords are concerned, the great attraction of using licence agreements (rather than granting tenancies) arises from the structure of the legislation.

Under the Rent Act 1977 a protected tenancy is "a tenancy under which a dwelling-house . . . is let as a separate dwelling." This formula has also been employed in section 1(1) of the Housing Act 1988, which sets out the basic definition of an assured tenancy. The full significance of this phrase is explained later. For present purposes, what is important is that statutory protection extends to tenancies (subject to various exceptions) but not to licences. Landlords (and their legal advisers) have therefore sought to employ the licence as a means of avoiding the application of the legislation.

Until quite recently, the courts were sympathetic towards landlords' granting residential licences instead of leases, provided that both parties understood the nature of the transaction. However, in the last few years, the House of Lords (the most senior court) has been critical of certain attempts by landlords to use licence agreements to get round the legislation. In a number of cases, the courts have concluded that the legal relationship between the landlord and the occupier is a tenancy, notwithstanding the fact that the landlord purported to enter a licence agreement.

The courts have not said that it is impossible for landlords to enter licence agreements. Indeed, many arrangements for the occupation of residential premises continue to be licences and not tenancies. The approach of the courts has been to decide that in certain circumstances an agreement – although superficially looking like a licence – is a sham or pretence, in reality being a tenancy.

the distinction between a lease (tenancy) and a licence

For a tenancy to exist it must satisfy two requirements:

○ it must be for a definite period of time
○ exclusive possession must be granted.

(Depending on whether the correct formalities have been satisfied in the creation of the lease, the tenancy will be either legal or equitable.)

for a definite period

The maximum duration of a fixed term tenancy must be known in advance. At the beginning of the second world war it became common to grant leases for the duration of the war. The courts took the view that such a grant was void at common law, because no one knew, at the time of the grant, when the war would end. Temporary legislation was passed to convert these arrangements into ten year leases, terminable by one month's notice by either party at the end of the war.

A lease will be regarded as satisfying the requirement of certainty of duration even though it contains provisions which mean that it may be ended prematurely. It would be rare to find a fixed term lease which does not allow the landlord to bring the lease to an end if the tenant fails to comply with his obligations under the lease, such as to pay rent. What is important is that the maximum duration of the lease is known in advance.

In relation to periodic tenancies, the maximum duration of the lease is not known in advance, since the arrangement between the landlord and the tenant continues until ended by agreement or notice to quit. However, the requirement of certainty of duration is satisfied as long as the period (week, month, year, depending on how often rent is payable) is definite at the beginning of the tenancy.

Uncertainty as to duration is unusual in the context of residential lettings. Where a lease is created by deed, or made in writing, the duration of the lease will normally be expressly stipulated. In less formal situations, a periodic tenancy will arise as a result of the payment of rent on a regular basis.

exclusive possession

Without exclusive possession there can be no lease, only a licence. A lease must give the occupier the right to use the premises as his home to the exclusion of all others, including the landlord. Most tenancy agreements have a clause giving the landlord the right to enter and inspect the condition of the premises, and possibly to carry out repairs (and even where no such right is expressly stated, the law may imply it). This does not affect the occupier's exclusive possession.

Where a person occupies premises as a licensee, however, the landlord retains control of the premises and has unrestricted access. A lodger, for example, is a licensee. A person is a lodger if the landlord provides attendance or services which require the landlord to exercise unrestricted access to, and use of, the premises. A lodger is an occupier of residential property, but he cannot call the place his own; he has no right to exclude the landlord; he does not have exclusive possession. The category of lodger includes hotel residents, a person living in an old-people's home, a student occupying a room in a hall of residence.

Although there can be no tenancy without exclusive possession, an occupier who has exclusive possession is not necessarily a tenant. It was decided by the House of Lords (in a case called *Street v Mountford*) that a person who has exclusive possession of residential premises for a definite period is a tenant unless the situation may be described as constituting exceptional circumstances. Such exceptional circumstances will arise in two situations:

○ Where the occupier's possession is referable to a relationship other than that of landlord and tenant, the occupier is a licensee

  for example: a purchaser who goes into possession of the property after exchange of contracts but before completion, and an employee who is allowed to live in his employer's premises for the better performance of his work are both licensees within this category.
○ A licence is created (notwithstanding the fact that the occupier has exclusive possession) if there was no intention by the parties to enter legal relations

  for example: where an owner as an act of generosity allows members of his family or friends to occupy residential premises, the arrangement will be classified as a licence.

shams

Where a person goes into occupation on the basis of a written contract which is phrased in terms of a licence, it used to mean that the occupier was a licensee. This gave landlords the go-ahead to use 'licences' as a means of avoiding the Rent Act 1977. In the case of *Somma v Hazelhurst*, for example, an unmarried couple were granted two separate agreements by Mrs Somma to occupy one bed-sittingroom. These agreements were couched in the terminology of licences (licensor, licensee, licence fee etc.) in order to make clear that there was no intention to create a tenancy. Moreover, the licences purported to deny exclusive possession, by the inclusion of a term permitting Mrs Somma to install other occupiers from time to time. The designed effect of the arrangement was that no tenancy was granted – either to one or to both of the occupiers. The Court of Appeal saw no objection to the arrangement and concluded that two licences had been created, and not a lease.

This approach has now been rejected by the courts. The House of Lords has made it clear that in a number of situations the courts will declare a licence agreement to be sham. The fundamental characteristic of a sham is that the form of the transaction disguises the substance. If the true substance of the agreement satisfies the conditions of a tenancy, by conferring on the occupier the right of exclusive possession for a definite period, then a tenancy will be created even though the agreement is phrased in terms of a licence.

In the context of licence agreements, three different types of sham can be distinguished: incorrect labels, smokescreen clauses, and interdependent agreements (moreover it is quite possible for all three types to arise in a single case).

incorrect labels
The first type of sham occurs when the terminology employed in an agreement misrepresents the legal category into which the arrangement falls. The courts will not be bound by the label attached to the agreement by the parties concerned.

In the case of *Street v Mountford*, the landlord purported to enter into a licence agreement with Mrs Mountford. Mrs Mountford signed an express declaration in the following terms: "I understand and accept that a licence in the above form does not and is not intended to give me a tenancy under the Rent Act". However, according to the terms of the agreement the landlord conceded that Mrs Mountford would have exclusive possession of the premises. The House of Lords held that Mrs Mountford was a tenant notwithstanding the declaration and the expressed intention of the parties not to create a tenancy. What was important was that under the agreement Mrs Mountford had a right to exclusive possession; therefore she was a tenant. Lord Templeman drew an analogy in the following terms:

"The manufacture of a five-pronged implement for manual digging results in a fork even if the manufacturer, unfamiliar with the English language, insists that he intended to make, and has made, a spade."

smokescreen clauses

Since the courts take the view that in principle an agreement which confers on an occupier the right of exclusive possession constitutes a tenancy, landlords have attempted to create licences by including within the terms of the agreements clauses which expressly negative the grant of exclusive possession. For example, clauses in the following terms have been employed by landlords in their attempts to prevent the occupier from being granted the right to exclusive possession:

- "The licensor shall be entitled at any time to use the rooms together with the licensee and permit other persons to use all of the rooms together with the licensee."
- "The licensor may for any reason and at any time require the licensee forthwith to vacate the flat and move to any other flat of comparable size in the building which the licensor may offer the licensee."

If clauses such as these are regarded by the courts as genuine, the occupiers will necessarily be licensees rather than tenants.

However, the courts will regard as sham, and therefore of no effect, clauses in an agreement by which neither party intends to be bound and which are obviously a smokescreen to cover the real intentions of both contracting parties. A smokescreen clause will arise in two situations.

First, if at the time of the agreement being made the landlord expressly states that a clause will not be relied upon, the courts will disregard it. For example, if a landlord or his agent on being questioned about the significance of a clause in a written agreement tells the prospective occupier that the clause is a 'legal formality', the court should regard the clause as sham. However, more often than not the prospective occupier – whose bargaining position is very weak – does not question the terms of the written agreement.

Secondly, a clause will be regarded as sham if it cannot be considered as seriously intended to form part of the substance of the relationship between the parties. This can be illustrated by a number of recent cases.

For example, in *Crancour v De Silvaesa* a couple moved into a bed-sittingroom under an agreement which purported to be a licence. According to the terms of the agreement, the occupiers were required to vacate the room with their possessions daily between the hours of 10.30 am and 12 noon. Also, the landlord had, under the agreement, an absolute right of entry to provide attendance and services, namely a housekeeper, to clean the room, to provide laundered bed-linen, and to remove rubbish. The judge in the county court decided that the occupiers were lodgers, and therefore licensees. The Court of Appeal, however, indicated that the terms of the agreement were 'astonishingly extreme' and this pointed to their being sham.

This approach has recently been confirmed by the decision of the House of Lords in *Antoniades v Villiers*. In this case, an unmarried couple occupied a flat which comprised kitchen, bathroom, bedroom and sittingroom. Each occupier had entered into a separate agreement with the landlord. Among the many terms which purported to negative the grant of exclusive possession, one (clause 16) provided that the landlord was entitled to share the flat with the licensee and to permit other persons to share the rooms with the licensee. When the landlord gave the occupiers four weeks' notice to quit they resisted, claiming that they were not licensees, but joint tenants protected by the Rent Act 1977.

The House of Lords declared the clause to be a sham, in spite of the intention of the landlord to create a licence, rather than a tenancy. In determining whether or not a clause is genuine, the expressed intention of the landlord (as evidenced by the terms of the agreement) was irrelevant; what was important was the surrounding circumstances. It was clear in *Antoniades v Villiers* that the landlord could not have intended the term about the sharing of occupation to be a true statement of the nature of the possession intended to be enjoyed by the occupiers. The flat was occupied by the couple, and the landlord could never have had any intention to occupy the premises himself. The clause did not have any practical operation or serve any purpose apart from the purely technical one of seeking to avoid the ordinary legal consequences of the landlord having let the occupiers into possession at a monthly rent.

Two points should be emphasised. First, where an agreement contains sham terms, the effect is not automatically to render the whole agreement null and void; the sham terms are struck out and the remainder of the agreement is examined to see whether exclusive possession is granted.

Accordingly, if any one of the terms which are included in the agreement in order to negative the grant of exclusive possession is genuine, the occupiers are not tenants. In a situation such as *Crancour v De Silvaesa*, for example, if the clause requiring the occupiers to vacate the premises for an hour and a half each day was a sham, but the terms giving the landlord unrestricted access to the premises in order to provide attendance and services was genuine, the occupiers would still have been licensees.

Secondly, particular problems arise in situations where residential premises are shared and each of the occupiers has entered a separate agreement with the landlord. If all the terms of the licence agreements which purport to deny the occupiers exclusive possession are sham there are still two possibilities of the agreement being a lease:

- ○ each occupier is a tenant of the part of the premises over which he has a right to exclusive possession (such as a bed-sittingroom)
- ○ the occupiers are joint tenants of the whole premises.

interdependent agreements

In *Antoniades v Villiers*, the House of Lords held that the couple occupying the premises were joint tenants. This was not an automatic consequence of the fact that the relevant clause was a sham, since even excluding sham clauses neither occupier individually enjoyed exclusive possession of any part of the premises. It was only by virtue of the fact that the licence agreements were interdependent, and therefore the rights of the occupiers were determined by reading the two agreements together (ignoring sham clauses), that the occupiers could be regarded as collectively enjoying the right to exclusive possession of the whole flat.

In cases involving shared accommodation the courts will not always regard the agreements as interdependent. For example, in *AG Securities v Vaughan* four occupiers shared a four-roomed flat (with kitchen and bathroom), which was held on a lease by the landlord. Each occupier had signed a separate agreement, clause 1 of which granted the right to use the flat in common with others who had or might from time to time be granted the like right. Unlike the couple in *Antoniades v Villiers*, the occupiers in *AG Securities v Vaughan* had signed the individual agreements and gone into occupation at different times.

The House of Lords did not see how a joint tenancy could be created by four separate documents of different dates in favour of four independent persons each paying a different rent and also for different periods of six months. Whereas in *Antoniades v Villiers* the two agreements were interdependent, the four agreements in *AG Securities v Vaughan* were independent. Since it had not been argued that each occupier had exclusive possession of part of the premises, the House of Lords was forced to conclude that the occupiers were licensees.

other dodges

Although the use of 'licence agreements' has been one of the most popular mechanisms for attempting to avoid statutory schemes of protection, landlords have also sought to exploit the express and implied exceptions to the legislation. However, where a landlord enters an artificial transaction in order to avoid the legislation, the courts may declare the arrangement to be a sham, in which case the tenant will have the benefit of the statutory protection.

holiday lets

Holiday lettings are not within the scope of statutory schemes of protection. Therefore, a landlord may seek to create an agreement which is not statutorily protected, by calling it a holiday let. Although in the past the courts have tended not to question the label employed by the landlord, more recently the courts have indicated that they will not be bound by the label employed by the parties to the agreement. Accordingly, where the description of a tenancy as a holiday let is wholly inappropriate, the courts will regard the arrangement as an ordinary tenancy. In one case it was held that a purported 'holiday let' for six months was not genuine since the landlord knew that the occupiers were student nurses and therefore were not occupying the premises for the purpose of a holiday.

the provision of board
Section 7 of the Rent Act 1977 provides that a tenancy is not a protected tenancy if the premises are let at a rent which includes payments in respect of board or attendance. Although in order to fall within this exception the board or attendance must account for a substantial proportion of the rent, in *Otter v Norman* the House of Lords held that the daily provision of a continental breakfast by the landlord was sufficient.

This exception applies only to tenancies under the Rent Act 1977, and there is no equivalent exception under the Housing Act 1988. Therefore, in relation to agreements entered into on or after 15 January 1989, a tenant will be an assured tenant under the Housing Act 1988 even if the landlord provides board. However, if the landlord provides attendance or services which require him to have unrestricted access to and use of the premises, the occupier will be a lodger (and therefore licensee) not a tenant.

company lets
Under the Housing Act 1988 it is provided that a tenant can only be an assured tenant if he is an individual and if he occupies the premises as his only or principal home. So, tenancies granted to companies appear to fall outside the scope of the Act.

A similar position arises in relation to tenancies entered into before 15 January 1989. Under the Rent Act 1977, when a contractual protected tenancy comes to an end, a statutory tenancy comes into existence. However, the 1977 Act provides that a statutory tenancy exists only as long as the tenant "occupies the dwelling-house as his residence." A company, therefore, cannot be a statutory tenant.

The 'company let' is a mechanism adopted by landlords with a view to exploiting this exception to the schemes of statutory protection. The most common form of company let is created in the following way:

○ the landlord refuses to let the premises except to a company
○ the prospective occupier purchases an off-the-shelf company (which costs in the region of £150)
○ the prospective occupier becomes the sole shareholder and director of the company
○ the premises are let to the company, which has the right to nominate the occupiers of the property
○ the company nominates the prospective occupier.

If this sequence of transactions is regarded as genuine, the occupier has no security of tenure since the company is the tenant and the company is not protected by the legislation.

The courts have tended to look favourably on company lets. There seems little doubt that where a tenancy is granted to a company which has an independent existence (rather than a company which has been expressly acquired for the purpose of becoming the tenant) the arrangement will be regarded as genuine. Furthermore, in a recent case it was held that a tenancy granted to an off-the-shelf company purchased by the sole occupier of residential premises was not a sham.

However, it is at least arguable that a tenancy granted to an off-the-shelf company is a sham. The approach of the House of Lords to the licence cases shows that the form of transactions should not be allowed to disguise the true substance of the arrangement. Where an off-the-shelf company is bought by the prospective occupier, the artificial nature of the series of transactions is transparent. If a company let is regarded as a sham, the true substance of the arrangement would be the grant of a tenancy to the occupier rather than the company.

ASSURED TENANCIES

An assured tenancy is the principal form of tenancy created by the Housing Act 1988. The majority of residential lettings granted after 14 January 1989 by private landlords will be assured tenancies. An assured tenancy is mainly distinguished from others by where the landlord lives and who he is. If he lives in another dwelling, or is a property company, the tenancy will almost always be 'assured'. In addition, for a tenancy to be assured, the tenant must pay a high enough rent, and the rateable value of the property must be within certain limits.

An assured tenancy gives to a tenant some degree of security of tenure and some degree of control over the rent he is asked to pay. The more important consequences of an assured tenancy are as follows:

○ The tenancy cannot be brought to an end by the landlord except by obtaining a court order or, in the case of a fixed term tenancy, by the landlord exercising an express power under a 'break clause' in the lease.

○ Possession cannot be obtained against the tenant without an order of the court, and the court may only grant an order for possession in prescribed circumstances.

○ The tenant must always be given notice of proceedings for possession by the landlord – that is, he must be informed that the landlord is applying for a court order.

○ The rent and other terms of the tenancy are principally a matter for agreement between the parties, but in certain specified circumstances either, or both, may be referred to a rent assessment committee. In any event the rent chargeable by a landlord will be an 'open market' rent.

○ On the death of a periodic tenant, the landlord may normally regain possession of the premises, but the deceased

tenant's spouse has certain rights of succession to the tenancy.
○ The court may order the transfer of an assured tenancy from one spouse to another when a decree of divorce or judicial separation is granted or at any time after that.

Assured tenants can enforce the rights generally available at law to all tenants, for example rights to repair, or to quiet enjoyment of their home, without risking eviction as a result of their actions. These general rights are discussed in the last chapter of this book.

what is an assured tenancy

Section 1 of the Housing Act 1988 says that

"A tenancy under which a dwelling-house is let as a separate dwelling is . . . an assured tenancy . . ."

This part of the definition of an assured tenancy mirrors the definition of a protected tenancy under the Rent Act 1977 and is likely to be construed by the courts in a similar way.

It has three component parts. There must be:

(i)   a dwelling-house
'Dwelling-house' has been interpreted widely by the courts to include a house or part of a house, a cottage, bungalow, maisonette or flat, a single room (for example a bedroom or bed-sit), even a beach-hut – in short, any premises which are capable of being lived in. Two flats let together as one dwelling have been held by the courts to constitute a dwelling-house; similarly a house and an adjacent cottage which were let together.

It must be intended at the time of the letting that the tenant should live in the accommodation. If the letting is for some other purpose, a shop for instance, then it is not an assured tenancy. Where premises are let for business purposes, the tenant cannot establish an assured tenancy simply by living in the property, unless the landlord consents to a change of use.

(ii)   *which is let*

The relationship of landlord and tenant must exist: there must be a tenancy. A mere licence to occupy cannot be an assured tenancy. Thus lodgers, caretakers and employees who have to occupy accommodation because of their job are excluded. It does not matter how the tenancy was created, whether by deed, written agreement or by word of mouth, nor whether it is a periodic tenancy or a tenancy for a fixed term.

(iii)   *as a separate dwelling*

The accommodation must be let as a single unit. One property may comprise several self-contained units let separately on assured tenancies. Two self-contained units (two flats, for example) can constitute one separate dwelling provided the tenant carries out all the normal activities of living in both (he cannot, for instance, just use one unit for sleeping in). The tenant must normally be able to sleep, cook and eat in the accommodation. But the fact that the tenant has to share bathroom facilities with others will not prevent an assured tenancy from arising. However, where any living accommo- dation – a sitting room or kitchen for example – in a property is shared, what is let is not a separate dwelling.

sharing

Section 3 of the Housing Act 1988 specifically deals with the situation where the tenant shares living accommodation with other tenants (this arrangement is outside the definition of an assured tenancy in section 1 because there is no 'separate dwelling'). Provided that the tenant has the exclusive use of some accommodation (a bedroom, for instance), section 3 gives him an assured tenancy of that accommodation and an inviolable right to use the shared accommodation during his assured tenancy.

However, if the tenant shares living accommodation with his landlord or with his landlord and others, section 3 does not apply. The tenant is not 'assured' and will only be able to rely on his rights under the general law.

Section 4 of the Act goes on to deal with the position where a tenant sub-lets part (but not the whole) of his dwelling-house. The tenant is not excluded from being an assured tenant merely because he shares living accommodation with his sub-tenant. (The sub-tenant is, however, excluded from being an assured tenant because he shares living accommodation with his landlord.)

tenant must be an individual

A tenancy which satisfies the above requirements will only be an assured tenancy if, and so long as, the tenant (or each of the tenants, if there is a joint tenancy) is an individual. 'Company lets' (where the tenant is a company) are therefore excluded from protection. Theoretically, the letting must genuinely be to a company and the occupier may challenge a 'company let' on the ground that its expressed purpose is a sham. To prove a sham, the occupier must show that in reality the accommodation was meant for him alone, not for employees generally (or a certain type of employees, such as company directors). In practice, however, the courts have shown a marked reluctance to castigate such tenancies as shams even in blatant cases of avoidance. In one recent case, an actress wanted to rent a flat in north-west London, which the landlord would only let to a company. She bought for £150 an off-the-shelf company, which then entered into a tenancy agreement with the land-lord. The agreement was signed by the actress as managing director of the company and she went into occupation of the flat, ostensibly under the terms of a rent-free licence from the company. When the landlord later brought an action to re-cover possession of the flat, the actress claimed that the agreement was a sham. The Court of Appeal held that the transaction was not a sham and granted the landlord an order for possession.

only or principal home
The third requirement for an assured tenancy is that the tenant (or in situations involving joint tenants, at least one of them) must occupy the dwelling-house as his only or principal home. Occupation is a question of fact and degree and may ultimately have to be decided by the court. A tenant who occupies only a part of the accommodation and sub-lets the remainder will satisfy the requirement.

By virtue of section 1(6) of the Matrimonial Homes Act 1983 (as amended by the Housing Act 1988), possession by the tenant's deserted spouse counts as occupation by the tenant. The landlord cannot refuse to accept rent from whichever spouse is in occupation. (This prevents the landlord bringing proceedings to end the tenancy on the ground of non-payment of rent.) However, this protection is not available to a tenant's ex-wife or ex-husband, nor can it apply to accommodation other than the matrimonial home.

exceptions

The letting will not be an assured tenancy if, and so long as, one (or more) of the following exceptions applies:

(1) If the tenancy was entered into, or the contract was made before 15 January 1989.
(2) If the rateable value of the property is above the rateable value limits laid down by the Housing Act 1988, namely £1,500 or less in Greater London, or £750 or less elsewhere. The local authority's valuation officer will help with enquiries relating to rateable values.

   Where the tenant's dwelling-house forms only a part of a property (and this part has not been valued separately for rating purposes) the rateable value of the whole will have to be apportioned. Similarly, where the tenant's dwelling-house consists of two separately rated properties, the separate rateable values will have to be aggregated. Any dispute relating to such apportionment or aggregation must be referred to a county court judge, whose decision is final.

No provision has been made in the 1988 Act for the introduction of poll tax in about 1991. It will of course be possible to ascertain the rateable value of older properties from existing valuation lists. But what about new properties? Presumably the government will bring out further legislation to deal with this point.

(3) If no rent is payable, or a low rent amounting to less than two-thirds of the present rateable value of the property. Payments in respect of rates, services, management, repairs, maintenance or insurance are to be disregarded for the purposes of this calculation unless such sums are expressed to be payable as rent. Tenants who are occupying accommodation under long leases (normally leases for over 21 years) will, as a rule, be excluded from being assured tenants because they pay little or no rent and a separate annual service charge.

It will be possible for an assured tenant to gain or lose the protection of the Housing Act 1988 if there is a change in the terms of his tenancy. One rather obvious, but effective, move of a landlord who wishes to rid himself of an assured tenant would be to offer to that tenant a new tenancy at a very low rent, namely less than two-thirds of the present rateable value. A tenant should obviously think very carefully before accepting such a seemingly attractive offer.

(4) If the premises are let for business purposes or mixed residential and business purposes.

(5) If part of the tenant's dwelling-house is licensed for the sale of intoxicating liquor for consumption on the premises. A publican letting a flat above his pub, however, can do so on an assured tenancy.

(6) If the dwelling-house is let together with more than two acres of agricultural land.

(7) If the dwelling-house is part of an agricultural holding and is occupied by the person responsible for the control of the farming of the holding.

(8) If the letting is by a specified institution to a student. Specified institutions include universities, colleges, polytechnics and other educational institutions, and bodies or foundations specifically established to provide accommodation for students. The exception covers rooms in halls of residence but not lettings by private landlords to people who happen to be students.

(9) If the purpose of the letting is to confer on the tenant the right to occupy the dwelling-house for a holiday, that is 'a period of cessation of work, or a period of recreation.' It has not yet been finally decided by the courts whether premises let for the purposes of a working holiday can come within the exception. The letting must be a genuine holiday let, not a sham – as, for example, a landlord letting premises for the purposes of a holiday when he knows the occupiers are student nurses. If the agreement contains a statement that it is a holiday letting, it would be up to the tenant to prove to the court that its expressed purpose is a false label.

(10) If the tenancy is granted by a resident landlord, that is one who occupies, as his only or principal home, the same house or flat as the tenant and has done so since the tenant moved in. Living in the same block of purpose-built flats (as against in the same flat) would not make him a resident landlord. But a landlord who occupied, as his only or principal home, another flat in a converted house would be a resident landlord. Where there are joint landlords (that is, where the tenancy has been granted by two or more persons together) it is sufficient if one fulfills the 'resident landlord' requirement. A company (that is, a company which owns and lets out premises) cannot be a resident landlord.

This exception will not apply where the tenancy is granted by the same landlord to a tenant who was previously an assured tenant of the same premises; for example, when a tenancy comes to an end and the landlord moves into the premises and then grants the tenant a new lease.

If a landlord ceases to be a resident landlord on a permanent basis, the tenancy becomes an assured tenancy under the 1988 Act. However, in the following two situations the letting will remain excepted from assured status even where the landlord is not resident:

- ○ If a resident landlord dies, two years are allowed for the winding-up of the estate. During this period, a person who has inherited the dwelling may decide to make it his home and so re-satisfy the resident landlord condition. Alternatively the personal representatives of the deceased landlord may exercise the ordinary common law rights of a resident landlord to obtain possession. If neither of these events occur within the two-year period, the tenancy becomes assured.
- ○ If the premises are sold and the buyer (the new landlord) gives the tenant notice within 28 days that he intends to occupy, as his only or principal home, the same house or flat as the tenant and he does so within six months.

(11) If the landlord is the Crown or a government department. Lettings by the Crown are, however, capable of being assured tenancies, if the property is managed by the Crown Estate Commissioners (which most Crown property is) and the letting does not fall within one of the other exceptions.

(12) If the landlord is a local authority, fully mutual housing association, newly-created housing action trust or any of the other similar bodies listed in the 1988 Act.

(13) If the letting is a transitional case, that is, one where a tenancy continues in its original pre-1989 form until phased out, namely:

- ○ a protected tenancy under the Rent Act 1977
- ○ a housing association tenancy
- ○ a secure tenancy.

(14) If the purpose of the letting is to provide temporary accommodation under the 'homeless persons' legislation: the exception lasts for only one year from notification to the tenant of the local authority's decision as to his housing status, or until the landlord notifies the tenant that he is an assured tenant.

'old-style' assured tenancies

Generally speaking, the Housing Act 1988 converts all 'old-style' assured tenancies, that is assured tenancies which were created under the Housing Act 1980, into 'new-style' assured tenancies (that is, the type of assured tenancies we are currently considering). This includes any 'old-style' assured tenancy granted by a fully mutual housing association before 15 January 1989, so long as that association remains the landlord. Tenancies granted by fully mutual housing associations on or after 15 January 1989 are excluded from protection under the 1988 Act. A fully mutual housing association is one which

- ○ limits its membership to its tenants or its prospective tenants; and
- ○ prohibits the granting or assignment (sale) of tenancies to persons other than members.

An outline of the scheme of protection which was afforded to 'old-style' assured tenants appears on page 126 of this book. No new 'old-style' assured tenancies can be created after 14 January 1989.

disputes

If there is any doubt whether or not an assured tenancy under the Housing Act 1988 has been created, either the landlord or the tenant may apply to the county court for a declaration as to the status of the letting. A tenant would be wise to seek legal advice before embarking on this course. Not only will he be putting his home at risk but, if the court finds against him, he will incur court costs. It may be better for him to await possession action by the landlord and then attempt to establish an assured tenancy as part of the defence.

when the landlord wants to end an assured tenancy

The Housing Act 1988 makes a distinction between contractual periodic tenancies and contractual fixed term tenancies.

landlord ending a contractual periodic assured tenancy
Section 5(1) of the Act provides that the only way in which a landlord can end a periodic assured tenancy is by obtaining an order of the court under the Act. Thus, a notice to quit (which is the normal way of ending a periodic tenancy) is totally ineffective. The periodic assured tenancy will continue automatically unless the court orders otherwise. Before the landlord can go to the court, he must serve on the tenant notice of proceedings for possession, in a prescribed manner. And the court can only grant an order for possession if the landlord shows that one of the grounds for possession laid down in the Act is satisfied.

landlord ending a contractual fixed term assured tenancy
Under the general law, a contractual fixed term tenancy will normally end only on expiry (that is when the term runs out). However, many fixed term tenancy agreements give the landlord power to bring the tenancy to an end in certain circumstances by forfeiture, or (less frequently) by notice to 'determine' (notice to quit).

But the 1988 Act provides that a fixed term assured tenancy cannot be ended by a landlord exercising a power of forfeiture in the lease. The tenancy will come to an end on expiry or, where applicable, if the landlord serves notice to quit. In addition, a landlord may end a fixed term assured tenancy by obtaining an order of the court under the 1988 Act. For this, the lease must contain a power for the landlord to end the tenancy (that is, a power of forfeiture or to serve notice to quit); the landlord must serve proper notice of proceedings for possession and he must establish one or more of the limited grounds for possession specified by the Act.

If, however, a fixed term assured tenancy comes to an end naturally, or is ended by the landlord otherwise than by obtaining an order of the court under the Act, then the landlord is not entitled to recover possession of the premises (even though the contractual fixed term has ended). Instead, the tenant is entitled to remain in possession of the premises under a **statutory periodic assured tenancy**, which is a periodic tenancy imposed by the 1988 Act. (The special terms of this statutory periodic assured tenancy are discussed at page 59.) This statutory periodic tenancy will not, however, arise if the tenant is granted by the landlord a new tenancy of the same or substantially the same premises.

landlord ending a statutory periodic assured tenancy

A statutory periodic assured tenancy cannot be brought to an end by the landlord except by obtaining an order of the court. (Again, a notice to quit is ineffective for this purpose.) The landlord must serve notice of proceedings for possession in the prescribed manner, and a possession order can only be granted by the court on specified grounds.

the grounds for possession

The circumstances under which a court must or may grant an order for possession are laid down in s. 7 and Schedule 2 of the Housing Act 1988. Grounds 1 to 8 (under Part I of Schedule 2) are mandatory; grounds 9 to 16 under Part II are discretionary.

If the landlord can show that one of grounds 1 to 8 under Part I applies, then the court must order possession. The court does not have to consider whether it is reasonable to make the order. In all other situations, the landlord must satisfy the court both that it is reasonable to make the order and that the circumstances are as specified in any of grounds 9 to 16 under Part II.

The 1988 Act gives no definition of the word 'reasonableness' but a similar requirement exists in connection with the discretionary cases for possession under the Rent Act 1977. Case law has established that in considering reasonableness, the court should take into account

○ the purpose of the legislation; in the case of the Housing Act 1988, this is to provide the tenant with some security of tenure but not to place insurmountable difficulties in the way of a landlord wishing to get possession
○ the personal circumstances of both parties, landlord and tenant, including their housing positions, their ages and health
○ the tenant's conduct under the tenancy
○ the severity of any breach of the tenancy agreement
○ public interest.

Where the tenancy is a periodic assured tenancy (whether contractual or a statutory periodic tenancy which has arisen on the ending of a fixed term tenancy) all of the grounds for possession are available to a landlord. If, however, the tenancy is for a fixed term which has not yet ended, the landlord may only apply to the court for an order of possession

(1) on grounds 2 or 8 under Part I, or any of the grounds under Part II, except grounds 9 and 16; and
(2) if the tenancy agreement states that the landlord can bring the tenancy to an end on the ground in question, for example by forfeiture or by giving notice to quit.

using the proper court

Any application by a landlord for a possession order under the Act should be made to the county court. Applications to the High Court are actively discouraged by providing that if costs are awarded to a landlord there, they should not exceed those he would have got if he had proceeded in the county court.

mandatory grounds for possession

The eight mandatory grounds are listed in Part I of Schedule 2 to the Housing Act 1988. If the landlord establishes any of these grounds, the court is obliged to grant him a possession order, irrespective of whether it thinks it reasonable to do so.

To be operative, grounds 1 to 5 require the landlord to have given "notice in writing to the tenant that possession might be recovered on this ground", no later than at the start of the tenancy. Such notice need not be in any particular form but it must state quite categorically that possession might be recovered under the particular ground. Where a landlord grants a succession of tenancies, of the same accommodation to the same tenant, one notice right at the start will do: a fresh notice does not have to be served on the grant of each new tenancy. This, of course, does not apply if there is a change of tenant or a change of premises.

For grounds 1 and 2, the notice requirement may be waived and a possession order granted by the court, provided it thinks it just and equitable to do so.

Once the court is satisfied that a landlord has the right to repossess the property on one of the mandatory grounds, it must make an order for possession; it has no power to adjourn the proceedings, or to postpone the date of possession.

Here are the eight mandatory grounds:

GROUND 1 *returning owner-occupier/landlord requires the property as a home for himself or his spouse*

Provided the landlord gave written notice to the tenant before the beginning of the tenancy that possession might be recovered under ground 1, the court will order the tenant to move out if it is satisfied regarding one of the following:

(a) that the landlord (or in the case of joint landlords, at least one of them) occupied the accommodation as his only or principal home at some time before letting it; or

(b) that the landlord (or in the case of joint landlords, at least one of them) requires the accommodation as his or his spouse's only or principal home. Part (b) can not be used by a landlord who buys premises with an assured tenant already in occupation, but it is available if he becomes the landlord in some other way, for example because he inherits the property, with a sitting tenant in it.

If it considers it just and equitable to do so, the court can still grant an order for possession in either case, even though the landlord did not serve the proper prior notice.

Ground 1(a) merely requires the property to have been occupied by the landlord as his only or principal home at some time before the letting. This enables a 'returning owner-occupier' to grant a succession of 'ground 1' tenancies without having to go back into residence before each. The minimum period of notice that must be given to a tenant where a possession order is sought on ground 1 is two months, so, on a practical level, a landlord might be well advised to retain (in the lease) one bedroom in the house or flat and a right of access to it; then when he returns from his absence abroad, he can at least have access to a room in the house while the possession proceedings are going ahead.

GROUND 2 *mortgagee seeking possession*

This ground applies where the landlord has mortgaged the property prior to granting the tenancy, has defaulted on the mortgage repayments or has broken some other term of the mortgage, and the mortgagee requires possession of the property in order to sell it with vacant possession. The landlord must have given the tenant notice in writing on or before the start of the tenancy that possession might be recovered on ground 2, but the court can waive this requirement if it thinks it just and equitable to do so.

GROUND 3 *out of 'holiday season' lettings*

This ground deals with the problem of what to do with holiday homes out of season. If the home was let on a fixed term tenancy of 8 months or less, having been let for a holiday during the previous 12 months, the landlord must be granted a possession order.

Suppose Mr Alexander has a seaside bungalow near Cromer which he lets out to holidaymakers during the season. From May to October he let the bungalow to Mr and Mrs Brown on a genuine holiday let. No one seems to want to spend money on a seaside holiday there during the winter, and instead of leaving the bungalow empty for the winter months, Mr Alexander decides to let the painter, Ms Cook, rent it. As long as he first serves Ms Cook with written notice that possession might be required under ground 3, and he does not grant Ms Cook a lease for longer than 8 months, he will be able to get a (mandatory) possession order from the court to get Ms Cook out again, because the bungalow was genuinely let for a holiday during the 12 months prior to the lease to Ms Cook.

GROUND 4 *out of 'student term' lettings*

This ground is similar to ground 3. It dovetails with exception 8 of the types of tenancies which cannot be assured tenancies, and allows accommodation owned by educational and other specified institutions to be let while it is not required for student use. The accommodation must have been let to the present short-term tenant, the tenant against whom the educational or other institution now wants to get possession, for a fixed term of 12 months or less, having been let to students during the previous 12 months, and prior written notice must have been given to the tenant that possession might be recovered on this ground.

GROUND 5 *clergy lettings*

The court must order possession if the accommodation was intended for a clergyman but was temporarily let to a lay tenant. The prior notice requirement must have been satisfied.

GROUND 6 *redevelopment*

This ground is available to a landlord who wishes to demolish or reconstruct the whole or a substantial part of the premises, or who wishes to carry out substantial works on the tenant's accommodation or on any part of it, or to the building of which that accommodation forms part. To ensure that this ground is not abused by landlords, a possession order will only be granted by the court if it is satisfied that it is not reasonably possible for the proposed work to be carried out without the tenant vacating the premises, because

(a) the tenant will not agree to new tenancy terms regarding access and other facilities, which are vital to the planned reconstruction or redevelopment; or
(b) the nature of the work means that the course outlined in paragraph (a) is, in any event, impracticable; or
(c) the landlord needs possession of part only of the tenant's accommodation in order to carry out the work (with, possibly, access etc. over the remainder), but the tenant is not willing to accept an assured tenancy of the remainder

(and/or to give the landlord the requisite rights of access etc. over the remainder); or

(d) such a tenancy of the remainder is, in any event, impracticable because of the nature of the work intended.

Ground 6 cannot be used by a landlord where the tenancy in question was formerly a tenancy protected by the Rent Act 1977 and has become an assured tenancy by virtue of the transitional provisions contained in the Housing Act 1988. Nor can the ground be used by a landlord who buys the premises with an assured tenant already in occupation.

If, despite the hurdles, a landlord does succeed in obtaining a possession order on ground 6, he must pay the tenant's reasonable removal expenses. This sum will be determined by the court if the landlord and tenant cannot come to an agreement.

GROUND 7 *death of former assured tenant*

This ground enables a landlord to get a possession order against a deceased assured tenant's relative(s) or other heir(s), within 12 months of the former tenant's death, or, if the court so agrees, within 12 months of the landlord first becoming aware of the former tenant's death. There is, however a limited exception in favour of a deceased tenant's spouse (which is explained at page 68).

The ground applies only if the tenancy was a periodic one (including a statutory periodic tenancy) when the former tenant died.

A landlord is not deemed to have created a new periodic tenancy merely because he accepts rent from whoever has inherited the tenancy during the 12-month or other period. If, however, there is a change in the terms of the former tenancy – for example, he increases the rent – he will then be deemed to have created a new tenancy and will be unable to recover possession on this ground.

GROUND 8 *serious rent arrears*

The landlord must be granted an order for possession if both at the time he serves notice of proceedings for possession and at the date of the hearing

○ at least 13 weeks' rent is unpaid if the rent is payable weekly or fortnightly; or
○ at least three months' rent is unpaid if the rent is payable monthly; or
○ at least one quarter's rent is outstanding three months after it was due if the rent is paid quarterly; or
○ at least three months' rent is more than three months in arrears if the rent is payable yearly.

discretionary grounds for possession

There are eight grounds on which the court may make an order for possession if it thinks it reasonable to do so.

All these grounds are available to a landlord where the assured tenancy is a periodic tenancy (either contractual or statutory). Grounds 9 and 16 are not available to a landlord where the tenancy is a fixed term contractual assured tenancy which has not come to an end.

In all cases, the court has discretionary power to adjourn proceedings, and if an order for possession is made, to stay or suspend the execution of the order or postpone the date of possession, for whatever period the court thinks fit. If the court does exercise its discretion in any of these ways, it may impose interim conditions on the tenant with regard to the payment of any rent arrears or the payment of future rent, and any other conditions, for example as to repair. Such conditions will not, however, be imposed if they would cause the tenant exceptional hardship. If the tenant breaks any condition imposed by the court, the landlord may apply to have any stay or suspension of the execution of an order, or any postponement of the date of possession, revoked.

The following are the discretionary grounds for possession (as listed in Part II of Schedule 2 to the Housing Act 1988):

GROUND 9 *Suitable alternative accommodation is available for the tenant or will be available for him when the order for possession takes effect.*

There are two ways in which a landlord can show the existence of suitable alternative accommodation. Firstly, he can produce a certificate from a local housing authority certifying that they are providing the alternative accommodation. Local authorities rarely give such certificates. Secondly, he can find and offer alternative accommodation himself. This accommodation will be suitable if

○ it is let as a separate dwelling on an assured tenancy (but not one in respect of which prior notice has been served that possession might be sought on one of grounds 1 to 5, or an assured shorthold tenancy); or
○ it is let as a separate dwelling on terms which give the tenant equal or equivalent security of tenure to the above; *and*
○ the court is satisfied that the accommodation fulfills certain specified conditions.

The specified conditions are

– that the accommodation is reasonably convenient as regards the tenant's and his family's place of work; and
– where appropriate, similar or suitable furniture is provided; *and either*
– the rent and size of the accommodation are that which a local housing authority or court would consider suitable for the needs of the tenant and his family; *or*
– the extent and character of the property is suitable to the tenant's and his family's needs.

This last condition was considered by the Court of Appeal in relation to the Rent Act 1977 in the case of *Hill v Rochard*, 1983. A retired couple were statutory tenants, under the 1977 Act, of The Grange, a period country house with a large number of rooms, servants' quarters, outbuildings, stables, a large garden and about one and a half acres of land. The landlords bought a four-bedroomed modern detached house with a garden and garage near to The Grange, and offered it as alternative accommodation to the couple. The offer was refused. The court granted an order for possession. In assessing the suitability of alternative accommodation, the court has to look at the tenant's needs, not his particular wishes and desires. The house clearly satisfied the couple's housing needs, if not their wishes.

However, a differently constituted Court of Appeal took a different view in *Battlespring Ltd v Gates*, 1983, in which an elderly widow was offered as alternative accommodation a similar flat to her present accommodation. But she had lived in her present flat for 35 years and had an emotional attachment to it and the Court of Appeal, agreeing with the county court judge, held that it would not be reasonable to make the order.

Where possession is sought on ground 9, the landlord must pay the tenant reasonable removal expenses. This sum will be determined by the court if necessary.

GROUND 10 *Some rent lawfully due from the tenant is unpaid when proceedings for possession are begun and was in arrears when notice of proceedings for possession was served on him* (except where the court has waived the notice requirement on just and equitable grounds).

The 1988 Act displays great concern with rent arrears and it remains to be seen how leniently or otherwise the courts will interpret the provisions.

The court has extensive powers to stay or suspend orders for possession on condition, for example, that the tenant pays off all arrears of rent.

Where the late payment is not the fault of the tenant, for example because of problems with the administration of housing benefit, it is possible that the court will not order possession.

GROUND 11 *Whether or not rent is in arrears at the commencement of proceedings for possession, the tenant has persistently failed to pay rent on time.*

The same comments as for ground 10 above apply to this ground.

GROUND 12 *The tenant is in breach of any of his obligations in the tenancy agreement, other than for payment of rent.*

Again, the court may, in an appropriate case, suspend the operation of an order for possession on condition that, for example, the tenant does the necessary repairs within a specified time.

GROUND 13 *The tenant has damaged the property or any of the common parts* (for example, hallways, stairs or lifts) *which he is entitled to use, or has allowed the same to deteriorate* (fair wear and tear excepted).

In the case of *Holloway v Povey*, 1984, an order for possession was granted against a Rent Act tenant who adamantly refused to mow the lawn and who let the grass grow uncontrolled.

GROUND 14 *The tenant has caused a nuisance or annoyance to neighbours* (not necessarily adjoining but in the near vicinity) *or has been convicted of using or allowing the premises to be used for illegal or immoral purposes.*

In general, the nuisance must be proved to be serious. Persistently playing loud music would constitute 'nuisance or annoyance', as would receiving late callers at frequent intervals. A conviction for receiving stolen goods or of being in possession of cannabis resin on the premises would be relevant under the second part of ground 14.

GROUND 15 *The tenant has damaged furniture* that was provided by the landlord (fair wear and tear excepted).

GROUND 16 *The tenant was an employee of the landlord* and the landlord now reasonably requires the accommodation for a new employee.

before the landlord can recover possession

Before a landlord can ask the court for an order of possession against an assured tenant, not only must he be able to establish one or more of the specified grounds for possession, but he must also serve on the tenant a 'notice of proceedings for possession' in accordance with section 8 of the 1988 Act. Section 8 expressly states that the court shall not entertain proceedings for possession unless such a notice has been served.

The notice must be in the prescribed form and specify the ground or grounds on which possession is sought and give particulars of such ground(s). It must also inform the tenant that proceedings for possession will not begin earlier than a certain specified date (this can be as soon as two weeks after the date of service of the notice). Further, the tenant must be told that those proceedings will, in any event, not begin later than twelve months from the date of service of the notice.

The notice form can be bought from law stationers.

length of notice
The length of notice to be given to the tenant depends on the type of assured tenancy (periodic or fixed term) and the ground(s) on which the landlord is seeking possession.

If the ground is, or includes any of grounds 1, 2, 5, 6, 7, 9 or 16, in Schedule 2, then the date specified in the notice as the earliest date for proceedings to start shall be:

○ in the case of a fixed term tenancy, two months (in any event, the court cannot grant a possession order on grounds 2, 9 or 16 during the continuance of an assured fixed term tenancy); or

○ if the tenancy is a periodic one (including a statutory periodic tenancy), either two months or the earliest date on which the tenancy could have been brought to an end under the general law by notice to quit, whichever is the later. So, for example, where rent is paid quarterly under a periodic tenancy, the earliest date would be three months from the end of the last quarterly period. But in the case of a weekly or monthly periodic tenancy, the date would be not earlier than two months from the date of service of the notice.

So, in any event, for grounds for possession 1, 2, 5, 6, 7, 9, 16, the minimum notice is two months.

Where an order for possession is being sought on grounds 3, 4, 8, 10 to 15, the earliest date for the start of proceedings to be specified in the notice is two weeks from the date of service of the notice.

The court can waive the requirement for notice of proceedings for possession to have been given, if it considers it just and equitable in the circumstances to do so. Failure to serve such a notice is not, therefore, necessarily fatal to a landlord's application for possession. It is unlikely, however, that the courts will dispense with the requirement easily, and never where a landlord is asking for a possession order on ground 8 (serious rent arrears).

compensation for misrepresentation

Where a landlord gets a possession order against an assured tenant and it is later discovered that he did so by misrepresenting or by concealing some material facts, the court may order the landlord to compensate the tenant for any loss the tenant has suffered through the order having been made against him.

when the tenant wants to end an assured tenancy

Where a tenant has a periodic assured tenancy, he must give the landlord at least four weeks' notice to quit, expiring at the end of a complete period of the tenancy (for example the end of a week if the tenancy is weekly). If the tenancy is a contractual periodic tenancy and provides for a longer period of notice to be given, the tenant must comply with this. A landlord may agree to a tenant leaving without giving notice.

The tenant of a contractual fixed term assured tenancy may only end the tenancy if the agreement allows him to do so (through a break clause) or if the landlord agrees.

the terms of an assured tenancy

These depend on whether the tenancy is a contractual fixed term assured tenancy, a statutory periodic assured tenancy, or a contractual periodic assured tenancy.

when it is a contractual fixed term assured tenancy

The parties are free to agree whatever terms they like, including rent. However, any term in the lease, or separate agreement between the landlord and tenant, which purports to prevent a statutory periodic assured tenancy coming into existence on the ending (otherwise than by an order of court) of a contractual fixed term assured tenancy, will be void.

Whenever a contractual fixed term assured tenancy ends, either naturally on expiry, or prematurely on termination by the landlord in accordance with a break clause in the lease, the tenant is entitled to remain in possession of the premises under the terms of a statutory periodic assured tenancy, unless he is granted a new lease of those premises.

when it is a statutory periodic assured tenancy

Such a tenancy is deemed

- to arise immediately the former fixed term tenancy has ended; and
- to be granted by the same landlord who granted the former fixed term tenancy; and
- to be of the same premises as the former fixed term tenancy; and
- to be for the same period as that for which rent was last payable under the former fixed term tenancy (for example, if the rent was payable quarterly under the former fixed term tenancy then the tenant will have a quarterly statutory periodic tenancy); and
- to be on the same other terms as the former fixed term tenancy, except that neither the landlord nor the tenant has any power to end the tenancy.

varying the terms of the agreement

A procedure is available whereby either a landlord or a tenant can propose a variation in the terms of a statutory periodic tenancy (i.e. one arising on the ending of a fixed term assured tenancy).

Within 12 months of the ending of the former fixed term tenancy and the statutory periodic tenancy arising, either party may serve notice on the other (called a 'section 6 notice', using Form DOE 16473) proposing a change in terms and a consequent adjustment of rent if desired. For example, under the fixed term agreement the tenant may have been responsible for internal decoration and now feels that the landlord should be responsible. The tenant may then serve the required notice on the landlord (or vice versa if the landlord wishes to propose a change).

A landlord can avoid this procedure altogether by granting the tenant a new lease immediately after the ending of a former fixed term assured tenancy, so preventing the statutory periodic tenancy from coming into existence. A landlord cannot simply increase the rent under this procedure; there must be new terms, for example as to the provision of furniture, which justify the increase.

The server (that is either, the landlord or the tenant) must specify in his 'section 6 notice' a date, not earlier than three months after the date of service of the notice, for the new terms (and rent, if any change is proposed) to come into effect.

the role of the rent assessment committee
If you receive such a 'section 6' notice and do not agree with the proposal then the matter may be referred to a rent assessment committee.

The referral must be made within 3 months in the prescribed form; the form is available from law stationers. It asks for details of the landlord and tenant and of the premises, what the current rateable value of the property is, whether or not services or furniture are provided, and who is responsible for repairs. A copy of the section 6 notice and of the tenancy agreement (if any) should be sent with the form.

The rent assessment committee will ask the parties whether they wish the matter to be decided by written or oral representations and they must reply to this within 7 days. (This period can be extended by the committee.) Where one or both of the parties wishes to make oral representations, the committee will arrange a time for him, or his representative (who need not be a solicitor), to be heard in person.

A rent assessment committee is normally made up of three people: a layman, a valuer and a lawyer who acts as president. They will consider the terms proposed and decide whether they, or some other terms dealing with the same subject matter, are such as one might reasonably expect to find in an assured periodic tenancy of the accommodation in question. The committee may do several things:

- agree that the proposed variation is appropriate
- decide that the proposed variation is not appropriate and confirm the original terms
- formulate other terms; these will be terms not in the original agreement which the committee consider might reasonably be expected to be found in an assured tenancy let on the open market.

Following the decision as to terms of the tenancy, the committee may then decide whether there should be any adjustment of rent, to take into account any variations made, and if so how much.

In arriving at their decision, the committee must disregard any effect on the terms (or the rent) attributable to the fact that the tenancy is granted to a sitting tenant.

Once a committee has reached a decision, the terms and any adjustment of rent determined by the committee become the new terms and rent of the statutory periodic tenancy. The committee will specify a date from which these terms are to start, which cannot be earlier than the date specified in the section 6 notice as the commencement date. The landlord and the tenant can, however, agree an alternative commencement date.

beware

If a section 6 notice is not referred to a rent assessment committee within three months of receiving it, then the terms (and any adjustment of rent) proposed in it automatically become the new terms of the statutory periodic tenancy from the date specified in the notice. The Housing Act 1988 thus provides dangerous scope for unilateral variation of the terms of a statutory periodic tenancy, and tenants in particular should be warned to act promptly on receiving a section 6 notice.

terms of a contractual periodic assured tenancy

As in the case of a contractual fixed term assured tenancy, the parties are free to agree whatever terms they like (including rent). However, a provision (whether express or implied) which allows a landlord to terminate the tenancy by serving a notice to quit will have no effect.

implied terms

In both statutory and contractual periodic assured tenancies, some important provisions are implied in the lease or agreement, even if they were not expressly stated.

assignment and sub-letting

Section 15(1) of the 1988 Act implies into every periodic assured tenancy a term that the tenant shall not, without the consent of the landlord, assign the lease (in whole or in part) or sub-let or otherwise part with possession (for example, allow a licensee into occupation) of the whole of the premises. (This does not prevent a tenant from sub-letting part without the landlord's consent unless his lease says otherwise.)

If a landlord refuses consent, the refusal cannot be challenged as being made on unreasonable grounds. It is, however, unlawful for a landlord to refuse consent to assign or sub-let because of the proposed assignee's or sub-tenant's race, or ethnic or national origin.

The term implied by section 15(1) can be excluded by an express term covering assignment or sub-letting etc, arising out of the 'section 6' procedure. It will also not apply where a contractual periodic assured tenancy expressly provides

○ that the tenant is not allowed to assign or sub-let, etc; or
○ that the tenant can only assign or sub-let etc. with the consent of the landlord (in this case the law requires that the landlord should not refuse his permission unreasonably); or
○ for a premium to be paid on the grant or renewal of the tenancy. For this purpose, premium is defined as a fine (that

is, a lump sum), any money payment in addition to rent, or a deposit which is more than one-sixth of the annual rent.

Where a landlord is expressly required to give his consent to assignment or subletting, the Landlord and Tenant Act 1988 states that he must consider any written application from the tenant promptly. If he withholds consent unreasonably or delays in responding, he must pay the tenant compensation.

access for repairs

Section 16 of the Housing Act 1988 implies into every periodic assured tenancy a term that the tenant will give the landlord access to the accommodation and reasonable facilities for the purpose of carrying out repairs. The implied term can be excluded if a term regarding access is added by the section 6 procedure.

increasing the rent under an assured tenancy

The initial rent level (and other terms of the tenancy) is that agreed by both the landlord and the tenant at the time of the tenancy agreement.

The procedure for setting future rent levels (and, where the Act allows, for a variation in the terms of a tenancy), depends on whether there is a mechanism for reviewing the rent within the tenancy agreement and on whether the assured tenancy is for a fixed term or periodic.

At common law, unless there is provision for it in the lease (lawyers call this a rent review clause), rent increases during the term can be demanded by the landlord only with his tenant's agreement. This common law rule applies to rent increases during a contractual fixed term assured tenancy. The amount of rent payable by such a tenant throughout the fixed term is that agreed at the outset of the tenancy. The rent may only be increased where there is a term in the lease allowing a review of the rent at specified times throughout the tenancy. Many professionally drafted fixed term leases do contain rent review clauses (but at present it is rare in a periodic tenancy of residential accommodation).

When the term expires, a statutory periodic tenancy will automatically arise (unless the landlord and tenant have agreed to enter into a new fixed term, or a new contractual assured periodic tenancy). Once a statutory periodic tenancy has arisen, the landlord may serve a notice on the tenant proposing an increase in rent under section 13 of the Housing Act 1988. The relevant form to be used is DOE 16477 *Landlord's Notice Proposing a New Rent under an Assured Periodic Tenancy*.

(If the landlord is also proposing to change the terms of the tenancy a different form, DOE 16473, has to be completed.)

The notice must indicate the date from which it is proposed that the new rent is to take effect. A tenant who agrees with the proposed rent need do nothing.

A tenant who disagrees and is unable to reach agreement with his landlord, or prefers not to discuss the matter directly with him, may refer the notice to the local rent assessment committee.

using the statutory review procedure

The notice must be referred to the rent assessment committee before the date indicated by the landlord. As with the procedure for varying the terms of a statutory periodic assured tenancy, the burden is on the tenant to act quickly. If he does not, he will be unable to challenge the increase in rent.

There is a special form for the tenant to use to which the landlord's notice is to be attached. This is form DOE 16478 *Application Referring a Notice Proposing a New Rent under an Assured Periodic Tenancy to a Rent Assessment Committee*. It asks, amongst other things, for a description of the premises and the terms of the tenancy (a copy of any written agreement should be included), details of any improvements carried out by the current or previous tenant(s) and whether or not services and furniture are provided and whether a premium (lump sum) was paid.

A copy of the tenant's notice will be sent to the landlord. Either party may be required to provide the rent assessment committee with more information. This will be sought on form DOE 16481 – failure to comply without reasonable cause is a criminal offence and may be liable to a fine. The parties will also be notified that they may send written submissions or request an oral hearing within a specified time.

When making any submissions, bear in mind that the committee is interested in, amongst other things:

– the state of repair of the property and any furniture or services provided
– the locality
– any information as to the level of rents (not 'fair rents') which are being charged for similar properties let on assured tenancies in the area. (This information can often be obtained from, for example, local newspaper advertisements, and letting agencies, and must be as up to date as possible.)

It is usual for a rent assessment committee to inspect the premises.

When it has received all this information, the rent assessment committee will, in accordance with the Act, decide on 'an open market rent' for the property. The committee has to assess from the information before them and using their own skill, knowledge and experience of rent levels for similar properties let on assured tenancies in the area, what rent a willing landlord might reasonably be expected to obtain for the property in question if let on the open market on an assured tenancy.

Their decision will be based on the assumption that the period and terms (other than rent) of this hypothetical letting are the same as those previously enjoyed by the tenant; that the hypothetical letting is to start on the date specified in the notice and that it is subject to any notices in connection with any of the mandatory grounds 1 to 5 for possession that the landlord has served. This latter assumption seems to suggest that a lower rent may be determined for such tenancies to reflect the lack of security of tenure.

The Housing Act 1988 also requires the committee to take into account any premium paid by the tenant and to disregard the following:

– any effect on the rent which can be attributed to granting the tenancy to a sitting tenant;
– any increase in value of the property attributable to improvements made by a tenant (except those carried out under an obligation in the lease);
– any reduction in value attributable to the tenant's failure to comply with the terms of the tenancy.

the decision
The rent determined will include an amount for any furniture provided by the landlord under the lease. It will also include any charges the tenant has to pay for services, repairs, maintenance or insurance, or management costs provided the charges are fixed. The rent will not include any charges which may vary due to cost. The rent determined may also include an amount for board where this is charged for under the lease (unless the amount is variable).

The decision of the committee will be sent to both parties and to the rent officer service.

The committee will not normally give reasons unless either the landlord or tenant has asked them to do so. (Although if reasons are requested immediately after their determination has been made the committee may provide reasons). These will normally be made in writing and copies sent to the parties either with the decision or shortly afterwards.

A copy of the committee's reasons for those properties where they have been requested are kept at the committee's office and are available on request, at a small cost.

There is no appeal on the facts decided by a rent assessment committee. An appeal on a point of law is provided by statute to the High Court or an application may be made for judicial review of the proceedings.

The rent determined will take effect as from the date specified in the landlord's notice, unless the committee have specified a later date to avoid hardship for the tenant.

This rent is the maximum rent that can be charged unless landlord and tenant agree that a higher or lower rent should be paid.

further rent increases

Once the rent has been increased, using the statutory procedure, no further rent increase may take effect until 12 months from the date of the previous increase (whether or not the rent assessment committee was involved in determining the rent).

withdrawing an objection

Once an application has been made to the committee there is no automatic right to withdraw if you change your mind. Withdrawal, is, however, likely to be allowed if both parties agree.

contractual periodic assured tenancies

The procedure for increasing the rent under a statutory periodic assured tenancy applies equally to a contractual periodic assured tenancy, BUT ONLY where the tenancy agreement contains no rent review clause. There are, however, the following differences:

- A landlord wishing to serve a notice of increase in rent on such a contractual periodic assured tenant will not be able to do so until the tenancy has been in existence for 12 months.
- The new rent takes effect at the beginning of a new period of the tenancy. This cannot be earlier than any of the following:

- ○ in the case of a yearly tenancy, 6 months after the landlord's notice was served
- ○ in the case of a period less than a month, 1 month
- ○ in any other case, a period equal to the period of the tenancy.

what happens when the tenant is no longer the occupier

On a former tenant's death, any assured tenancy will pass to those entitled to it under his will or on his intestacy. Provided that the person who has inherited the tenancy occupies the accommodation as his only or principal home (and the tenancy has not become excluded by one of the exceptions), the tenancy will remain assured. However, in the case of a periodic assured tenancy (contractual or statutory), a landlord has a mandatory right to a court order for possession (under ground 7) against such a person, to be exercised within one year of the former tenant's death. No such mandatory right to recover possession exists in relation to fixed term assured tenancies.

spouse's right to succeed to periodic assured tenancy

Section 17 of the Housing Act 1988 provides a limited exception to these rules in favour of a deceased periodic assured (including statutory periodic assured) tenant's spouse. On the tenant's death, the contractual periodic or statutory periodic assured tenancy will pass to the deceased tenant's spouse, provided he or she occupied the accommodation as his or her only or principal home immediately before the former tenant's death. The tenancy will not pass to anyone else under the former tenant's will or intestacy, nor will the landlord be able to recover possession of the premises under ground 7.

For the purposes of section 17, 'spouse' includes a so-called 'common law' wife or husband, but not a partner of the same sex. Any dispute between a spouse and a 'common law' husband or wife as to who is the successor 'spouse' will have to be decided by the county court.

There is no right of succession for a spouse where the tenant who has now died was himself a 'successor', that is where he became the tenant by virtue of section 17 or inherited the tenancy; or at some time before his death he was a joint tenant of the accommodation and became solely entitled to the tenancy by virtue of the right of survivorship. He will also have been a 'successor' if he became entitled to the tenancy because he was a successor under the transitional provisions relating to the phasing out of regulated tenancies under the Rent Act 1977.

A former tenant will also have been a 'successor' where, at some time before the grant of the tenancy in question, he was a successor (as defined above) to a previous tenancy of the same accommodation.

divorced or separated spouse
Under the Matrimonial Homes Act 1983, the court has power on granting a decree of divorce, nullity or judicial separation, or at any later time, to make an order transferring an assured tenancy from one spouse to the other.

Where the very existence of the assured tenancy depends on the deemed occupation rules (because the tenant-spouse is no longer occupying the accommodation as his or her only or principal home) the occupying non-tenant spouse must apply for a transfer order before decree absolute, because afterwards the deemed occupation rules no longer apply (as there is no marriage), the tenancy will lose its assured status and there will be nothing for the court to transfer.

The landlord has a right to be heard by the judge at the time of divorce (but no right of veto), and the needs of the non-tenant spouse (and children) must be balanced against the position of the landlord; his objections will be overridden if necessary. The court's jurisdiction under the 1983 Act does not apply to unmarried couples or to premises that were never intended to be the matrimonial home.

when there is sub-letting

An assured tenant can sub-let unless the terms of his tenancy forbid it. It is normally a condition (either express or implied) that the landlord's consent be obtained to any sub-letting. A tenant who ceases to occupy the premises as his only or principal home loses his assured status and the protection of security of tenure under the Housing Act 1988. But this, of course, does not prevent the sub-tenant being an assured tenant; he will not be excluded from protection unless one of the exceptions applies to his tenancy.

The general rule is that if a head tenancy of premises comes to an end, any sub-tenancy of the whole or any part of those premises comes to an end too. This is not so, however, where the whole or any part of premises are lawfully sub-let on an assured tenancy. Under section 18 of the Housing Act 1988, if the head tenancy comes to an end (by possession proceedings against the head tenant or otherwise – for example, if the head tenancy is a non-assured fixed term tenancy which expires) the lawful assured sub-tenancy does not come to an end. Instead, the sub-tenant of the whole or of any part is deemed to hold his tenancy directly from the head landlord on the same terms as if the head tenancy had continued. It makes no difference that the head tenant is not himself an assured tenant. Thus, suppose A lets premises to B company (lettings to companies cannot be assured tenancies) and B company lawfully sub-lets the premises on an assured tenancy to C. B company's lease comes to an end. C is entitled to remain in possession of the premises under his assured tenancy which is now directly held from A.

Section 18 will not operate if the head landlord could not have granted an assured tenancy. So, in our example if A was a local authority, section 18 cannot save C's tenancy. Nor can section 18 change a sub-tenant's rights: all it does is put him into a direct relationship with the head landlord if the head tenancy ends. Suppose, then, that the lawful sub-tenant was not an assured tenant, because the head tenant was a resident landlord. If the head tenancy ends, section 18 does not alter his rights or lack of them. Even though the head landlord is not resident, he is still not an assured tenant and has no security of tenure.

ASSURED SHORTHOLD TENANCIES

The assured shorthold tenancy is is the other form of tenancy created by the Housing Act 1988. It is a variant of an assured tenancy which should prove popular with private landlords because it provides them with an automatic right to repossess the property at the end of the term.

An assured shorthold tenancy will probably start life as a short term letting; it must initially be for a fixed term of not less than six months. But because, after that term has expired, it may continue as a statutory periodic tenancy for as long as the landlord wishes, it is possible that many assured shorthold tenancies will turn out to be very long-term arrangements.

The normal rights available to an assured tenant are also available to an assured shorthold tenant.

Any dwelling that can be let on a normal assured tenancy can be let on an assured shorthold. Basically this means that any private landlord can let furnished or unfurnished accommodation to a tenant on assured shorthold – provided that he fulfils certain conditions, namely

○ the tenancy must be for a fixed term of not less than six months; and
○ the tenancy must not contain a power for the landlord to end the tenancy during the first six months (this does not include a power of re-entry or forfeiture for breach of any term of the tenancy); and
○ prior to the grant of the tenancy, the landlord must have given the tenant a notice, in the form prescribed by statute, stating that the tenancy is to be an assured shorthold tenancy; and

○ the tenant must not have been, immediately before the grant of the tenancy, an assured tenant of the landlord (this does not prevent a succession of assured shorthold tenancies being granted to the same tenant, as explained below).

If any of these conditions are not complied with, the tenancy will be an ordinary assured tenancy.

rent

An assured shorthold tenant who feels the rent payable is substantially higher than that being charged for similar tenancies in the area may apply to a rent assessment committee at any time during the initial term of the tenancy for the rent to be reduced. He can do so provided that:

– the rent under the tenancy has not already been determined by a rent assessment committee, or
– the tenancy in question is the original shorthold tenancy and not a subsequent tenancy arising or granted (by the same landlord) on expiry of the earlier tenancy. (The rent fixing arrangements for a subsequent tenancy are the same as those which apply to assured tenancies and depend on whether the subsequent tenancy is a fixed term or periodic one.)

At the end of the fixed term the tenant can apply to the rent assessment committee only where the landlord issues a 'notice of increase'.

The tenant must complete a special form (DOE 16480) *Application to an RAC for a determination of a rent under an Assured Shorthold Tenancy*, a copy of which will be sent to the landlord.

The form asks for the address and other details of the accommodation, the name of the landlord, what the current rateable value of the premises is, whether the tenant received the proper assured shorthold notice before the tenancy was granted (a copy of the notice should accompany the application), whether the tenant paid a premium (a lump sum) for the tenancy, details of any services and service charges, whether furniture is provided, details of repair obligations, whether the tenancy is assignable (can be sold) and whether a premium is payable on assignment, and what is the existing rent (inclusive or exclusive of rates).

Before determining a rent, the committee members will have to satisfy themselves

– that there is a sufficient number of similar properties in the area let on assured tenancies (whether shorthold or not) to provide evidence of a market rent, and
– that the evidence indicates that the rent in question is substantially above the market level.

If either party has any evidence of these matters this should be put to the committee.

The rent assessment committee will assess a rent for the premises which they consider to be an open market rent for an assured shorthold in the locality. They will assume that the shorthold is for the same period and on the same terms as the one under consideration. No account will be taken of the fact that there is a sitting tenant in the premises. Any increase in value due to the tenant's improvements (other than those that he was obliged by the lease to carry out) must be disregarded, as must any decrease in value attributable to the tenant's failure to comply with the terms of the lease. A rent determined by the committee is exclusive of rates.

As assured shorthold tenants have no security of tenure and at the end of the term the landlord may obtain possession, it seems likely that a market rent for such tenancies will be less than the rent obtainable under an assured tenancy where the landlord can only get possession on certain grounds.

The open market rent will be the maximum rent that can be charged. No increase is allowed until 12 months after the date of the determination.

The committee will fix a date from which the new rent becomes payable. This date cannot be earlier than the date of the application. If the rent determined by the committee is less than the contractual rent, that new rent is the most the tenant can be charged.

The Secretary of State may, by order, exempt certain parts of the country from these rent regulation provisions.

Rent assessment committees have to keep proper records of all rents under assured tenancies (including assured shortholds) referred to them. These records can be inspected by the public. A charge of £1 is made for copies.

other terms

The position is the same as with contractual fixed term assured tenancies, that is, the parties have complete freedom of contract.

if the landlord wants to regain possession during the fixed term

The landlord can recover possession of the premises on the mandatory grounds 2 and 8 of Schedule 2 to the 1988 Act (mortgage default on the part of the landlord and serious rent arrears on the part of the tenant) and all the discretionary grounds for possession except grounds 9 and 16 (suitable alternative accommodation available for the tenant, and tenant ceasing to be employee of landlord) but only if the tenancy makes provision for it to be brought to an end on the ground in question. (In other words, the position is the same as for contractual fixed term assured tenancies.) Thus, where a landlord grants an assured shorthold for a fixed term he must ensure that there is provision in the lease for him to end it by forfeiture or re-entry on the tenant's breach of covenant, or other appropriate ground.

the landlord's choices at the end of the fixed term

Section 21 of the Housing Act 1988, gives the landlord the right to possession at the coming to an end of the fixed term, provided that

○ he has not granted the tenant a new contractual assured tenancy (whether shorthold or not); and

○ he has given the tenant at least two months' notice stating that he requires possession of the premises. This notice can be given to the tenant either before or on the last day of the tenancy.

Provided the landlord has fulfilled the conditions for creating an assured shorthold, has not granted the tenant a new assured tenancy, and has given the proper notice of intention to repossess, the court must grant an order for possession against the tenant. Such an order, once granted, takes effect immediately.

If, on the other hand, the landlord wishes to continue with the assured shorthold arrangement, he has three choices:

(1) he can allow the tenant to remain in possession under a statutory periodic assured shorthold tenancy, which arises automatically on the ending of the fixed term; or

(2) he can grant the tenant a new contractual fixed term tenancy; or

(3) he can grant the tenant a new contractual periodic tenancy.

All these tenancies will be assured shorthold tenancies, notwithstanding that the three conditions for the creation of an assured shorthold have not been fulfilled, unless prior to the start of the new tenancy the landlord serves notice on the tenant that the tenancy is not to be an assured shorthold. (If the landlord does this, he will lose his automatic right to possession under section 21 and the tenancy will be an ordinary assured tenancy.)

if the tenant remains in possession under a statutory periodic assured shorthold tenancy

In almost every respect, the rights of the parties during the new shorthold term are the same as if the tenancy was a statutory periodic assured tenancy. The landlord and tenant, of course, remain the same; the period of the tenancy is that for which rent was last payable under the fixed term; and the terms of the tenancy are the same as under the prior fixed term, except that any provision allowing either the tenant or the landlord to end the tenancy is excluded.

rights of the parties during the new statutory periodic assured shorthold term

Either the landlord or the tenant may use the section 6 procedure (to serve a notice of variation of the terms of the tenancy on the other), and that other may refer the notice to a rent assessment committee and ask them to determine the terms.

Similarly, the landlord may serve a notice on the tenant under section 13, to increase the rent, and the tenant may then refer his notice to a rent assessment committee. Where, however, the rent was determined by a committee during the prior fixed term under section 22, a landlord may not serve a section 13 notice on the tenant until after the first anniversary of that determination. A tenant may not refer his rent to a rent assessment committee under section 22 during a statutory periodic assured shorthold tenancy.

The terms implied by sections 15 (about assigning and subletting) and 16 (allowing access for repairs) into periodic assured tenancies (unless excluded) also apply in this case.

During the statutory periodic tenancy, all the grounds for possession in Schedule 2 are available to the landlord, provided he follows the correct procedure. In addition, because the statutory periodic tenancy is an assured shorthold, the landlord has a right to possession under section 21. This time, though, the date on which possession is required, specified in his notice of intended repossession, must be

○ the last day of a period of the tenancy; and
○ not earlier than two months from the date of the notice, or the date on which the tenancy could, at common law, be
brought to an end by notice to quit, whichever is the later.

if the tenant is granted a new contractual fixed term tenancy

The tenancy need not fulfil the assured shorthold conditions.

The terms of the fixed term tenancy are a matter of agreement between the parties. The tenant has no right to refer his rent, under section 22, to a rent assessment committee.

During the fixed term, grounds 2 and 8 and all the discetionary grounds for possession, except grounds 9 and 16, are available to the landlord, provided the tenancy contains provision for premature ending by the landlord on the ground in question. The landlord is additionally entitled to possession on the ending of the fixed term under section 21. He must not grant a new contractual tenancy, and he must serve, on or before the last day of the fixed term, at least two months' notice on the tenant stating that he requires possession.

If, however, at the end of the fixed term tenancy, the parties are happy to continue the shorthold arrangement, the cycle begins again.

if the tenant is granted a new contractual periodic tenancy

Again, the tenancy need not fulfil the shorthold conditions.

The parties are free to agree whatever terms they like. The implied terms in sections 15 and 16 (assigning/sub-letting and access for repair) will apply, unless excluded. The tenant has no right to ask a rent assessment committee to consider his rent under section 22, but the parties may avail themselves of the section 13 procedure (landlord's notice of increase, followed by referral of the notice by the tenant to a rent assessment committee for determination of the rent, provided that the tenancy agreement does not contain a rent) review clause.

A notice to quit will be ineffective to end the tenancy. The landlord must get an order for possession from the court if he wants the tenant to leave. All the Schedule 2 grounds for possession apply. The landlord can also use section 21 to repossess the premises. He must serve notice on the tenant requiring possession, no earlier than:

○ the last day of a complete period of the tenancy; or
○ two months from the date of the notice or the date on which the tenancy could, under the general law, be brought to an end by notice to quit, whichever is the later.

divorce and death

The position is exactly the same as for ordinary assured tenancies. The Matrimonial Homes Act 1983 deemed occupation rules, and power of the court to transfer the tenancy on divorce, etc., can all be used by the non-tenant spouse.

When a contractual fixed term assured shorthold tenant dies, the tenancy will pass to those entitled under his will or on his intestacy. If the deceased tenant was a statutory periodic assured shorthold tenant, or a contractual periodic assured shorthold tenant, his or her spouse generally has a right to succeed to the tenancy.

The landlord retains his right to repossess the premises under section 21 against a successor spouse.

TENANCIES IN EXISTENCE IN JANUARY 1989

The coming into force of the Housing Act 1988, on 15 January 1989, marked the end of an era for renting and letting in the private sector.

In the White Paper which preceded the Act, the government stated its intention to revive the private rented sector (in 1986 it represented only 8% of the total housing stock), citing 'too much preoccupation since the war with controls' as the chief reason for its decline.

This preoccupation had been embodied for the past decade in the main provisions of the Rent Act 1977. These gave 'regulated tenants' security of tenure, which was capable of spanning three generations, and a 'fair rent' system, which severely restricted the financial return a landlord could obtain from letting his property.

phasing out regulated tenancies

The general rule laid down by section 34 of the Housing Act 1988, is that no new regulated tenancies under the Rent Act 1977 can be created after 14 January 1989. Most new tenancies will be either assured or assured shorthold tenancies under the Housing Act 1988.

Regulated tenancies in existence before 15 January 1989 continue to be governed by the Rent Act 1977. They will gradually be phased out through the succession provisions imported into the 1977 Act by section 39 and Schedule 4 of the Housing Act 1988. But it will be many years before regulated tenancies completely disappear.

The majority of residential lettings granted by private land-lords before 15 January 1989 were regulated tenancies. Here is an account of the nature of a regulated tenancy, and the protection afforded to a regulated tenant.

nature of a regulated tenancy

A regulated tenancy may be either protected or statutory. It must start its life as a protected tenancy. It is protected while the original tenancy agreement (which need not be in writing and may be for a fixed term or periodic), is in existence. When the protected tenancy comes to an end, provided the tenant goes on living in the accommodation, what is known as a statutory tenancy will arise and the tenant will be entitled to remain in possession unless and until the court orders other-wise.

what is a protected tenancy?

Section 1 of the Rent Act 1977 defines a protected tenancy as: "A tenancy under which a dwelling-house (which may be a house or part of a house) is let as a separate dwelling".

This phrase also forms the basis of the definition of an assured tenancy under the Housing Act 1988 (see page 36).

The definition requires that the tenancy be of a separate dwelling. This does not cover the situation where the tenant has the exclusive use of some accommodation (a bedroom, for instance), but shares some living accommodation with others (for example, a sittingroom or kitchen – but not a bathroom: a shared bathroom doesn't count).

If the tenant shares living accommodation with other tenants, then section 22 of the Rent Act 1977 gives him a protected tenancy of his exclusive accommodation and the right to use the shared accommodation. But if he shares living accommodation with his landlord, or with his landlord and others, section 22 does not apply. The tenant may, however, have a restricted contract (dealt with later in the book from page 122 onward).

If the tenant does not have the exclusive use of any accommodation, he is a licensee and has no protection other than under the general law.

exception to being a protected tenancy
The letting will not be a protected tenancy if one (or more) of the following exceptions applies:

(1) If the letting is granted on or after 15 January 1989, unless:
  ○ the letting is entered into through a contract made before 15 January 1989; or
  ○ the letting is granted to an existing protected, or statutory tenant by the same landlord (or one of joint landlords). It does not matter that the new letting is of other accommodation belonging to the landlord; or
  ○ the letting is granted through an order for possession made by the court against a protected or statutory tenant on the ground of available suitable alternative accommodation, and the premises are those proffered in the proceedings, and the court directed that the new letting would be protected because an assured tenancy would not give the required security.

(2) If the rateable value of the property is above the rateable value limits laid down by the Rent Act 1977. The way in which the limits are defined by section 4 of the Act is complicated, but broadly speaking a property will be within the rateable value limits if its present rateable value is £1,500 or less in Greater London, or £750 or less elsewhere. If the present rateable value of a property is higher than this, it may still come within the rateable value limits if its rateable value on the valuation list which

expired on 31 March 1973 was £600 or less in Greater London, or £300 or less elsewhere.

(3) If no rent is payable, or a low rent of not less than two-thirds of the rateable value of the property on the 'appropriate day'. The appropriate day is either 23 March 1965 if the property was rated at that time or, if not, the date on which it became rated. In this context, rent means the whole rent payable to the landlord, including rates and quantified service charges. Long leaseholders (that is, those whose lease is for 21 years or more) are usually excluded from being protected tenants because they pay little or no rent; their payments for rates, services, maintenance or insurance are disregarded for this purpose.

A protected tenant may lose the protection of the Rent Act if there is a change in the terms of his tenancy. He would therefore be well advised to resist any proposal made by his landlord to reduce his rent significantly, or to grant him a new lease at a low rent, despite the obvious attractiveness of such a proposal.

(4) If part of the tenant's dwelling-house is licensed for the sale of intoxicating liquor for consumption on the premises. A publican letting a flat above his pub, however, can do so on a protected tenancy.

(5) If the rent includes payment for board or attendance - but only if the payment for attendance forms a substantial part of the rent.

Board means 'prepared food served on the premises'. An early morning cup of tea would not count. Nor, it seems, would a meal served in another building. But in a recent case, the House of Lords decided that a continental breakfast which was available daily in the basement dining room of the house constituted board.

Attendance means 'services personal to the tenant' and would include cleaning rooms, doing laundry and changing bed-linen, but not the cleaning of communal parts such as entrance halls and stairways.

(6) If the letting is by a university, college or polytechnic to one of its students, or by some other body specified by regulation. The bodies are all educational institutions and foundations specifically established to provide accommodation.

(7) If the purpose of the letting is to give the tenant the right to occupy the dwelling for a holiday. Holiday means 'a period of cessation of work, or a period of recreation'. As yet, the courts have given no definitive ruling on whether premises let for the purposes of a working holiday can come within the exception. The letting must genuinely be a holiday let; the court is astute to detect a sham. But it is up to the tenant to establish a sham; the landlord is not required to prove that the expressed purpose ('holiday') is the true purpose.

(8) If the property is let for business purposes, or for mixed residential and business purposes.

(9) If the landlord is a local authority, a registered housing association, or a housing co-operative.

(10) If the landlord is a government department. Lettings by the Crown, however, are capable of being protected tenancies, provided the property is managed by the Crown Estates Commissioners (which most Crown property is) and the letting does not fall within one of the other exceptions.

(11) If the letting is an 'old style' assured tenancy.

(12) If the letting was granted after 14 August 1974 by a resident landlord. A resident landlord is one who lives in the same house or flat as the tenant and has done so from the time the tenant moved in. Living in the same block of purpose-built flats (as against in the same flat) would not make him a resident landlord. But a landlord living in another flat in a converted house would be a resident landlord. A company landlord (that is a company which owns and lets out premises) cannot 'reside'. Although a resident landlord must be resident in the property at the

time of the letting, he may have more than one home and need not occupy any one of them continuously. But he must always intend to return and use the property as a home and show visible signs of that intention, such as leaving clothes there.

Before 1974, the distinction was between furnished and unfurnished tenancies, rather than resident and non-resident landlords. Furnished tenancies were excepted from protection. It may be necessary to decide whether a tenancy created before August 1974 was furnished or unfurnished. If it was unfurnished, the presence of a resident landlord will not exclude it from protection.

The resident landlord exception does not apply if the letting is to an existing protected or statutory tenant of the same dwelling.

landlord ending a protected tenancy

If the tenancy can be ended by notice to quit, either because there is an express term to this effect or because the tenancy is a periodic one, at least four weeks' notice in writing must be given to the tenant. The period of notice will have to be longer if the lease so requires, or if the tenancy period is for more than four weeks. A notice to quit a periodic tenancy must expire at the end of a complete period of the tenancy (for example at the end of the month, if monthly) unless the tenancy agreement states otherwise.

form of notice to quit

A notice to quit must contain the following prescribed information (in the following recommended form of words):

"1. If the tenant does not leave the dwelling the landlord must get an order for possession from the court before the tenant can be lawfully evicted. The landlord cannot apply for such an order before the notice to quit has run out.

2. A tenant who does not know if he has any right to remain in possession after a notice to quit runs out, can obtain advice from a solicitor. Help with all or part of the cost of legal advice or assistance may be available under the Legal Aid Scheme. He should also be able to obtain information from a citizens advice bureau, a housing aid centre, or a rent officer.''

Standard *Notice to Quit a Dwelling* forms are available from law stationers.

When a protected tenant receives a notice to quit he does not have to get out there and then. His protected tenancy will end on the day the notice to quit runs out, but a statutory tenancy will arise in its place. The tenant need not leave unless and until the landlord has obtained an order for possession from the court.

if a fixed term tenancy

It would be rare for a short residential fixed term tenancy to have a break clause allowing the landlord to end it by 'notice to determine'; the lease comes to an end automatically on the specified date, and cannot be ended sooner. But most fixed term leases contain a provision allowing the landlord to forfeit the lease if the tenant fails to pay the rent or breaks any of his other covenants. (Some periodic leases also contain a forfeiture clause, although this is unusual. Since notice to bring a periodic agreement to an end is so easy to give, such a clause would be rarely, if ever, used.)

A landlord must first serve the tenant with a 'section 146' notice before proceeding to forfeit the lease for breach of covenant other than non-payment of rent. And whatever the breach (non-payment of rent or otherwise), the landlord must get a court order for forfeiture. The tenant has the right to apply to the court for relief against forfeiture.

Even if a court order for forfeiture is obtained by the landlord, he still cannot recover possession. He must also prove that he can get possession on one of the 'cases' under the

Rent Act. (Often, though, the tenant's breach will also amount to a ground for possession.) A statutory tenancy comes into existence on the ending of the fixed term, and the tenant cannot be made to move out of his home unless and until the landlord obtains a court order for possession.

what is a statutory tenancy?

A statutory tenancy can only arise when the protected tenancy that preceded it is properly ended (determined), provided that none of the above 12 exceptions applies.

A statutory tenancy only lasts for as long as the tenant continues to occupy the premises as a residence. This is because a statutory tenancy confers merely a personal right to remain in residential occupation unless and until the landlord gets a court order for possession on one of the limited grounds set out in the Rent Act. As a consequence, a statutory tenant cannot normally assign (that is, sell) or sub-let the whole of the premises. (Also, if a statutory tenant goes bankrupt, the trustee in bankruptcy gets nothing because the tenancy is not assignable, and the tenant is entitled to remain in his home. This is in contrast to the situation where a protected tenant goes bankrupt: the original agreement is still in existence and the tenancy passes to the trustee in bankruptcy and the tenant may have to move out.)

This residence requirement does not mean that a statutory tenant can never leave his home, and it is recognised that a person can have more than one home. The tenant cannot be compelled to spend 24 hours in all weathers under his own roof 365 days a year. Clearly, for instance, the tenant of a London house who spends his weekends in the country, or his long vacation in Scotland does not necessarily cease to be in occupation. A tenant, with a house in the country, who stayed in his flat twice a week, but rarely ate a meal there, succeeded in his claim to a statutory tenancy.

Generally speaking, the tenant must at all times use the

accommodation as his home and, if away, always intend to return and leave visible signs of that intention, such as clothes, furniture or a member of his family with whom he normally resides. A tenant who left his flat to care for his seriously ill parents, but always maintained a wish to return to the flat permanently, retained his statutory tenancy. In another case, however, a statutory tenant of a flat went to live with his girlfriend, although he left clothes and furniture in his own flat and used the flat during the day to work (he was a writer); he lost his statutory tenancy.

By section 1(6) of the Matrimonial Homes Act 1983, where either a husband or wife is entitled to occupy accommodation by virtue of a statutory tenancy, as long as the other spouse is there it counts as occupation by the tenant for the purposes of keeping the statutory tenancy alive. The landlord cannot refuse to accept rent from whichever spouse is in occupation. (This prevents the landlord bringing proceedings for possession on the ground of non-payment of rent.) However, this protection does not apply to divorced or unmarried couples, nor to accommodation other than the matrimonial home.

terms of a statutory tenancy

A statutory tenancy will be on the same terms and conditions as the protected tenancy that preceded it, so far as they are consistent with the provisions of the Rent Act. Thus, covenants as to quiet enjoyment, repair, and prohibitions against sub-letting continue to bind the statutory tenant. The main types of inconsistent terms and conditions are those which relate to recovery of possession or which permit assignment or sub-letting of the whole of the premises with the landlord's consent.

ending a statutory tenancy

A landlord cannot end a statutory tenancy, except by obtaining a court order for possession. No notice to quit need be given to the tenant.

company tenants

A company can be the tenant under a protected tenancy, there being no requirement that the tenant be an individual. A company cannot, however, be a statutory tenant because it is incapable of residing and it cannot rely on the residence of one of its employees (or other occupier) for this purpose. As a result, a company tenant can claim Rent Act protection as far as rent is concerned, but cannot claim security of tenure for either itself or for a resident occupier.

'Company lets' (where the tenant is a company) have been used by landlords as a means of avoiding the Rent Act. Theoretically, a resident occupier may challenge a 'company let' on the ground that its expressed purpose is a sham; that is, that the parties' real intentions were to let to the resident occupier and that the 'company' was no more than a nominal tenant.

before a dispute arises

If there is any doubt whether or not there is a protected or statutory tenancy, either the landlord or the tenant may apply to the county court for a declaration as to the status of the arrangement. A tenant would be wise to seek legal advice before embarking on this. If the court finds against him, not only will he be putting his home at risk, but he will incur court costs. It may be better for him to await a possession action by the landlord and then attempt to establish a protected or statutory tenancy as part of the defence.

when the landlord wants to get back the property

Court proceedings for possession will fail unless the landlord can prove

○ that the protected tenancy has been properly ended (no notice to quit is needed for a statutory tenancy, however long it has been in existence); and
○ that he is entitled to possession on one of the grounds for possession set out in the Rent Act.

the grounds for possession

The circumstances under which a county court may or must grant an order for possession are laid down by law, in section 98 and Schedule 15 to the Rent Act 1977 (as amended by the Housing Act 1980 and the Rent (Amendment) Act 1985).

Most of the statutory grounds for possession are called 'cases'. Cases 1 to 10 under Part 1 of Schedule 15 are discretionary (case 7 was abolished by the Housing Act 1980); cases 11 to 20 under Part 2 are mandatory.

If the landlord can show that one of cases 11 to 20 under Part 2 applies, then the court must make an order for possession. The court does not have to consider whether it is reasonable to make the order.

In all other situations, the landlord must satisfy the court both that it is reasonable to make the order and that either:

– suitable alternative accommodation is available; or
– the circumstances are as specified in any of cases 1 to 10 under Part 1.

reasonableness
The Rent Act gives no definition of the word reasonable but

case law has established that in considering reasonableness the court should take into account

○ the purpose of the Rent Act, which is to confer security of tenure
○ the personal circumstances of both parties, landlord and tenant, including their financial and housing positions, their ages and health
○ the tenant's conduct under the tenancy, for example whether rent payments are regular or irregular
○ the severity of any breach of covenant
○ public interest.

suitable alternative accommodation

The court may make an order for possession if it is satisfied that it is reasonable to do so and that suitable alternative accommodation is available to the tenant, or will be available to him when the order for possession takes effect.

The two ways in which a landlord can show that there is suitable alternative accommodation are firstly by producing a certificate from a local housing authority certifying that they are providing the alternative accommodation. Local authorities rarely give such certificates, however. Secondly, he can find and offer alternative accommodation himself. This accommodation will be suitable if

○ it gives the tenant equal or equivalent security of tenure; and
○ it is reasonably convenient as regard the tenant's and his family's place of work; and
○ the rent and size of the accommodation are what a local authority or court would consider suitable for the needs of the tenant and his family; and
○ where appropriate, similar or suitable furniture is provided; and
○ the extent and character of the property are reasonably suitable to the tenant's means and to his and his family's

needs. How this requirement was considered by the Court of Appeal in *Hill v Rochard*, 1983 and by a differently constituted Court of Appeal in *Battlespring v Gates*, 1983, is described on page 54 of this book.

A letting of suitable alternative accommodation granted after 15 January 1989 will normally be an assured tenancy. However, where an order for possession is made on this ground against a protected or statutory tenant, a court may, in the course of proceedings, direct that the suitable alternative accommodation be held on a protected tenancy, if it considers that an assured tenancy would not afford the tenant the required security. It remains to be seen whether the courts will equate assured and protected tenancies for this purpose. In any event, it is important that tenants and their representatives in suitable alternative accommodation cases do all they can to ensure that the court directs that the new tenancy should be a protected one. Arguments for this would include that the increased rent under an assured tenancy means that the alternative accommodation is not suitable to the tenant's needs and/or that it is unreasonable to make the order.

discretionary grounds for possession

The cases in which the court may make an order for possession if it thinks it reasonable to do so but where no alternative accommodation is offered, are as follows:

CASE 1
The tenant has not paid the rent or is in breach of one of his other obligations in the tenancy agreement – for example, to carry out repairs.

The court can suspend the operation of an order for possession on condition, for example, that the tenant pays off all arrears of rent, or does the necessary repairs.

(The order to pay off arrears should only be made if it would not cause exceptional hardship to the tenant; tenants on income support can argue that exceptional hardship would be caused.)

CASE 2

The tenant has caused a nuisance or annoyance to neighbours (not necessarily adjoining but in the near vicinity) *or has been convicted of using the premises for illegal or immoral purposes.*

Generally speaking, the nuisance must be serious. Making excessive and persistent noise would constitute 'nuisance and annoyance', as would overfilling your bath at frequent intervals and letting water escape into a downstairs flat. A conviction for receiving stolen goods or of being in possession of cocaine or 'smack' on the premises would be relevant under the second limb of case 2.

CASE 3

The tenant has damaged the property or allowed it to deteriorate (except for fair wear and tear).

In *Holloway v Povey*, 1984, where an order for possession was granted to a landlord against a tenant who adamantly refused to mow the lawn and who let the grass grow uncontrolled, the order was suspended on condition that the tenant would tidy up the garden and keep it tidy for one year.

CASE 4

The tenant has damaged furniture that was provided by the landlord (fair wear and tear excepted).

CASE 5

The tenant gave notice to quit (but subsequently changed his mind) and in consequence of the notice the landlord has contracted to sell or let the property.

The landlord would need to show that it would cause him financial loss if the tenant were not leaving.

CASE 6
The tenant has assigned or sub-let the whole of the property without the landlord's consent.

This is only appropriate to a protected tenancy; a statutory tenant who assigns or sub-lets the whole of the property ceases to be protected by the Rent Act.

CASE 8
The tenant was an employee of the landlord and the landlord now reasonably requires the accommodation for a new employee.

CASE 9
The landlord reasonably requires the property as a home for himself or a member of his immediate family.

To grant an order for possession under this case, the court must be satisfied that greater hardship would be caused by refusing the order than by granting it.

The landlord has to show that he reasonably requires the property as a home for himself or a member of his family and that it is reasonable to make the order for possession; it is up to the tenant to show greater hardship. All the relevant circumstances are taken into consideration in deciding whose would be the greater hardship, including: availability of other accommodation, financial status, health, other people who would be affected (for example dependants), length of time the tenant has lived in the area, job and school connections in the area, and so on.

The court may make an order for future possession, as it did where a 62 year old landlord wanted possession of a tenanted cottage so she would have somewhere to live on her mother's imminent death.

Case 9 is not available at all to a landlord who bought the premises with the protected or statutory tenant already in occupation, but is available if he became the landlord in some other way, for example because he inherited the property with a sitting tenant in it.

CASE 10
The tenant has charged a sub-tenant a higher rent than is permitted.

This applies only where there is a rent registered for the premises, or part of them, with the rent officer or by a rent tribunal.

mandatory grounds for possession

These are listed in cases 11 to 20 in Part 2 of Schedule 15 to the Rent Act 1977. If the landlord establishes any of the grounds detailed in these ten cases, the court is obliged to grant him an order for possession, irrespective of whether it thinks it reasonable to do so.

To be operative, each case requires the landlord to have given 'notice to the tenant that possession might be recovered under this case', no later than the start of the tenancy (or before the grant of the tenancy in the case of a protected shorthold; this is dealt with later, at page 118 onward). Such notice need not follow any particular form but it must state quite specifically that possession might be recovered under the particular case. This notice requirement may be waived and a possession order granted by the court in cases 11, 12, 19 and 20 provided the court thinks it just and equitable to do so.

There is a special procedure enabling landlords to get possession quickly under cases 11 to 20. The county court office can advise on how to do this. A tenant faced with such proceedings has to act fast if he wishes to oppose the landlord's application: the period between his receiving the court papers and the hearing will be at the most 14 clear days, instead of the usual 21, and in some cases may be as little as 7 clear days.

Once a mandatory order for possession is made, it cannot be postponed for more than 14 days except on the ground of exceptional hardship. If there is exceptional hardship, the court can postpone the order for up to six weeks. Exceptional hardship is a question of fact in each case – for example, if the tenant or a member of his family has some special need, perhaps a physical disability which necessitates special accommodation so that it may take a little longer than two weeks to find somewhere to live.

Here are the ten mandatory cases.

CASE 11 *returning owner-occupier*

This case is designed to enable a person temporarily to let his home. Provided the landlord lived in the accommodation at some time before letting it and, from the start of that tenancy and previous tenancies, gave written notice to the tenant that possession might be recovered under case 11, the court will order the tenant to move out if it is satisfied regarding one of the following:

○ the owner-occupier or any member of his family who was living with him when he last occupied the accommodation, wishes to live in it; or

○ the owner-occupier has died and a member of his family who was living with him when he last occupied the accommodation (or another house) wishes to live in it; or

○ the owner-occupier has died and the person who has inherited the property either wants to live in it or to sell it with vacant possession; or

○ the property is subject to a mortgage granted before the tenancy, and the lender wishes to exercise his power of sale (for example, because repayments have not been made); or

○ the owner-occupier wants to sell the property with vacant possession in order to buy a home nearer his workplace.

It is not necessary for the landlord to have lived in the accommodation immediately before the letting. Therefore, a landlord who occupied the property as his residence some years before the present tenancy, or who granted a succession of case 11 tenancies culminating in the present one without going back into residence before each, will be entitled to possession, provided the other conditions are satisfied.

And if it considers it just and equitable to do so, the court can still grant an order for possession, even though the owner did not serve the proper notice.

An owner-occupier does not have to be a freeholder: a tenant who is entitled to sub-let the whole of his home under his agreement can also use case 11 to get possession from his sub-tenant.

CASE 12 *intended retirement home*
This case can be used by people who let a home to which they plan to retire. The owner must intend to live in the accommodation when he retires from regular employment and must have given the tenant notice in writing, on or before the start of the tenancy, that possession might be required under case 12. If the owner has previously let the property, it must also have been under case 12. The court must order the tenant to give up possession if it is satisfied that

○ the owner has retired from regular employment and wants to use the property as a retirement home; or
○ the owner has died and a member of his family who was living with him at the time of his death, wants to live in the property; or
○ the owner has died and a person who has inherited the property either wants to live in it or to sell it with vacant possession; or
○ the property is mortgaged and the lender wishes to exercise his power of sale.

The court may waive the requirement that proper notice must be served or that any previous letting must have been under case 12.

CASE 13 *out of 'holiday season' letting*
Where the home was let for a fixed term of 8 months or less, having been let for a holiday during the previous 12 months, the landlord must be granted a possession order.

CASE 14   *out of 'student term' letting*
This case covers accommodation let by educational and other
specified institutions during student vacations. The accommodation must have been let to the present short-term tenant, the
one against whom the institution now wants to get possession,
for a fixed term of 12 months or less, having been let to
students during the previous 12 months.

CASE 15   *clergy letting*
The court must order possession if the accommodation was
intended for a clergyman but temporarily let to a lay tenant.

CASE 16   *farmworker letting*
Similarly, possession will be granted to a farmer who has let
property that was formerly occupied by a farmworker to an
ordinary tenant on a temporary basis.

CASE 17   *farmhouse letting*
This applies where a landlord requires a farmhouse not previously occupied by a farm manager following amalgamation
proposals.

CASE 18   *farm manager letting*
This case covers the situation where the accommodation was
previously occupied by a farm manager or his widow and has
been let temporarily to an ordinary tenant.

CASE 19   *shorthold tenancies*
(Shorthold tenancies are dealt with separately later in the
book.)

CASE 20   *lettings by servicemen*
This case is similar to cases 11 and 12: where a person was a
member of the armed forces when he bought and let the
property, and the tenant and any previous tenant was given
notice on or before the start of the tenancy that possession

might be recovered under case 20, the court must grant an order for possession if it is satisfied that

○ the serviceman wants to live in the property; or
○ the serviceman needs to sell the property with vacant possession to buy a home nearer his work; or
○ a member of his family who was living with him at the time of his death, now wants to live in the property; or
○ a person who has inherited the property either wishes to live in it or sell it with vacant possession; or
○ the property is mortgaged and the lender wishes to exercise his power of sale.

The court may waive the 'proper notice' requirement if it thinks it just and equitable to do so.

statutory overcrowding
The court will also grant an order for possession if the property falls within the definition of being overcrowded under Part 10 of the Housing Act 1985.

when the tenant wants to end a regulated tenancy

How a tenant can do this depends on whether the regulated tenancy is protected or statutory. If the tenancy is still protected and is a

○ **periodic tenancy** – the tenant must give the landlord at least four weeks' notice to quit, expiring at the end of a complete period of the tenancy (for example, the end of the month if the tenancy is monthly). The notice must be in writing but no special form is required. If the tenancy agreement provides for a longer period of notice to be given, the tenant will have to comply with this.
○ **fixed term tenancy** – the tenant may only end a fixed term

tenancy prematurely if either the agreement or the landlord allows him to do so.

If the tenancy has become statutory, the tenant must give the landlord at least four weeks' notice to quit in writing, but more if the original agreement required longer notice to be given. Where the original tenancy was for a fixed term, the tenant must give at least three months' notice in writing irrespective of the length of the original term. There is no special form for a tenant's notice to quit a statutory tenancy. Again, the landlord may agree to the tenant leaving without giving notice.

divorced and separated spouses

Under the Matrimonial Homes Act 1983, the court has power on granting a decree of divorce, nullity or judicial separation, or at any later time, to make an order transferring a protected or statutory tenancy from one spouse to the other.

Where the very existence of the statutory tenancy depends on the 'deemed occupation' rules, it is essential that the occupying spouse applies for a transfer order before the decree absolute, because that decree will bring the statutory tenancy to an end.

The landlord has no right of veto, merely a right to be heard by the judge at the time of the divorce, and the needs of the non-tenant spouse (and children) must be balanced against the position of the landlord; his objections will be overridden if necessary. The court's jurisdiction under the 1983 Act does not extend to unmarried couples, or to premises that were never intended to be the matrimonial home.

sub-letting

A regulated tenant can sub-let unless the terms of his tenancy forbid it. But a statutory tenant can only sub-let part because if he ceases to reside in the premises, he loses the statutory tenancy and the protection of the Rent Act.

If a tenant sub-lets on a regulated tenancy, he must give his landlord written notice of the sub-letting within 14 days and include details of the occupancy and the rent.

The normal rule is that if a head tenancy of premises is brought to an end, any sub-tenancy of the whole or part of those premises ends too. This is not the case where a regulated tenant creates a lawful sub-tenancy of the whole or part of a dwelling-house. Under section 137 of the Rent Act 1977, if the regulated head tenancy is ended by possession proceedings, the sub-tenant of the whole or any part is deemed to hold directly from the head landlord as if the regulated head tenancy had continued. If the landlord wants possession against the sub-tenant he must bring a separate action.

For section 137 to apply, the sub-tenant must himself have been a regulated tenant; section 137 cannot change his rights – all it does is put him into a direct relationship with the head landlord if a possession order is obtained against the head tenant. Suppose, that the lawful sub-tenant was not a regulated tenant because the head tenant was a resident landlord, if the head tenancy is ended, section 137 does not alter his rights. Even though the head landlord (now his immediate landlord) is not resident, he is still not a regulated tenant and has no security of tenure.

rent control

The Rent Act 1977 contains a mechanism for the registration of what is known as a fair rent, for a dwelling which is the subject of a regulated (protected or statutory) tenancy.

A fair rent is one assessed by a rent officer or, on appeal, a rent assessment committee, in accordance with the rules laid down in section 70 of the Rent Act 1977. Once assessed, the rent is entered in the rent register which is kept by the rent officer and is open to public inspection free of charge if you go in person (if you want to obtain a copy of an entry on the rent register the fee is £1). By looking at rents registered for similar dwellings in the area, a landlord and a tenant can get an idea of the fair rent attributable to their accommodation.

getting a fair rent registered

Either the landlord or the tenant of any regulated (protected or statutory) tenancy, or both of them, may apply to the local rent officer for a fair rent to be registered. The address of the local rent officer is in the telephone directory.

Application is made on a standard form (RR1), available from the rent officer, law centres, citizens advice bureaux, and housing aid centres. The form is easily completed and asks, amongst other things, for details of the landlord and the tenant, a description of the premises and the terms of the tenancy (a copy of any written tenancy agreement should be included), whether any services or furniture are provided and whether a fair rent has previously been registered for the premises.

The rent (including an amount for services and/or furniture provided by the landlord, but exclusive of rates) which the applicant seeks to have registered must be entered on the form. If no rent is specified, the rent officer cannot deal with the application. If the applicant is the landlord and any services are provided, he must also give details of the costs. A copy of the application is sent to the tenant.

The parties will usually be invited to consult with the rent officer. Before their meeting, the rent officer may inspect the premises.

The rent officer then decides on a fair rent. Section 70 of the Rent Act requires that in so doing he should have regard to the character, state of repair and locality of the dwelling and, if the tenancy is furnished, the quality and condition of the furniture. He should disregard any value arising from a shortage of similar rented accommodation in the area. The value of any improvements made or paid for by the tenant (other than those he was obliged by his lease to carry out) should also be disregarded, as should any disrepair attributable to the tenant's failure to perform his repairing obligations. The personal and financial circumstances of the landlord and tenant must not be taken into account.

A rent officer's usual method of assessment is the 'comparables' method – that is, using as a starting point fair rents already registered for similar accommodation in the area.

The resulting fair rent will be registered usually within 12 weeks after the initial application was received. Both parties will be sent a copy of the registration sheet showing the new rent and notes outlining the effects of the registration.

the service element

A registered rent reflects the cost of any services provided by the landlord – for instance, cleaning and lighting of common parts, gardening. Details of the cost of any services have to be entered on the application form. They must be accompanied by a schedule showing how these figures are arrived at and the method of apportionment between occupiers, if more than one tenancy; they can be challenged by the tenant. If a 'fixed' fair rent is registered, the part of it attributable to services is noted separately (unless it is less than 5% of the total rent) and so is any increase in the cost of services since the previous registered rent.

Sometimes a tenancy agreement provides that the landlord may vary service charges payable. If the rent officer approves this provision, he will register a rent which reflects, but does not always detail, the current cost of services, and will simply state that the fair rent is 'variable'. This means that a landlord can recover the actual amount expended on services for any particular period of time. How this amount is split among different flats in a block depends on the agreement between the landlord and the tenants. It may be split pro rata according to the size of each flat, or just split equally.

The Landlord and Tenant Acts 1985 and 1987 give important protection to a tenant who has to pay a variable service charge and this is described at page 241.

no rates element

A registered rent does not include rates. If the landlord pays the rates he cannot recover them from the tenant unless the tenancy is statutory or the tenancy agreement so provides. In any other case, the landlord will have to wait until the protected tenancy has ended before he can begin to charge for rates. A periodic protected tenancy can be ended by notice to quit. However, instead of the landlord having to serve both this and a demand for rates, the law allows him to serve a 'notice of increase of rates' which fulfils both purposes. The length of the notice (that is the date of the increase) must be the same length as for a notice to quit and cannot be backdated. When the notice has expired, the periodic protected tenancy ends and a statutory tenancy comes into being. From then on, the landlord can charge for rates.

certificate of fair rent

There was a procedure whereby precautionary applications could be made by landlords contemplating improvements to, or the letting of, accommodation so that they might discover in good time whether it would be worth their while in rental terms. They could ask the rent officer to fix a fair rent for the premises and insert this in a certificate. Provided the improvements were carried out, or the accommodation was let, within two years of the certificate, the landlord could apply to have the fair rent in the certificate registered.

Since 15 January 1989 a certificate of fair rent cannot be applied for by a landlord. But certificates applied for before that date remain unaffected.

taking the case to the rent assessment committee

If the landlord or the tenant is dissatisfied with the rent registered, he may (within 28 days of receiving notification of the registration) object in writing and ask to have the case considered afresh by a rent assessment committee. A committee is normally made up of a layman, a valuer and a lawyer. They will assess a rent for the premises which they deem fair at the time of their decision – but they too are bound by section 70 of the Rent Act 1977.

An objection cannot be made if a joint application was made by the landlord and the tenant and the rent officer determined, without further consultation, that the rent specified in the application was a fair one.

When an objection is received by the committee, both parties are supplied with information about procedure, and of any arrangements made to hold a hearing. They may both be asked if they wish to make oral or written representations. There will be a hearing unless the parties notify the committee that they wish the matter to be dealt with on written representations. There is a time limit (usually 7 days) for replies. The rent officer's papers on the case which were not sent to the parties previously will accompany the letter. At this stage, the committee may ask either party to supply further information. There is a fine if this is not done within 14 days.

If no hearing has been requested (either by the committee or the parties), both parties are given an opportunity to comment on each other's written representations. The committee nearly always inspects the premises before making a decision.

the hearing
If a hearing has been requested, or is ordered by the committee, the parties will be given about 10 days' notice of its date, time and venue. Hearings are open to the public and are quite informal; the parties may speak for themselves or get someone else to represent them.

In order to acquaint the committee fully with the arguments, both parties (landlord and tenant) will be asked to state what they think the rent for the premises should be, and why. Relevant points may include the size, age and locality of the dwelling, its state of repair and any furniture and services provided. The shortage of rented accommodation let on the same terms as the regulated tenancy in the area will not be considered by the committee, and the financial and personal circumstances of the parties cannot be taken into account. The tenant will be given the opportunity to question the landlord, and vice versa. The committee may also question the parties, and witnesses may be asked to speak.

the decision

The committee's function is a simple one. They have to confirm the rent officer's figure if they think it is fair. If not, they have to determine a fair rent themselves which may be higher or lower than the rent registered, and may be fixed or variable (if the lease allows for variation). They sometimes give their decision at the hearing but more often it is communicated through the post. The committee need not give reasons for their decision unless one of the parties asks them to do so before the hearing. (Also, at the discretion of the committee, reasons may be given if requested within a reasonable time after the decision has been received by the parties.) The decision is also sent to the rent officer who will mark the register accordingly.

There is a right to appeal to the High Court against a committee's decision on a point of law, but the High Court cannot determine a fair rent for the premises. Alternatively, leave to apply for judicial review may be sought to quash the committee's decision – for instance where there is evidence that no reasonable committee could have come to the decision they did, and/or that irrelevant matters were considered or relevant matters not considered.

withdrawal of objection

When a matter has been referred to a rent assessment committee, either party may withdraw his objection if the other party and the committee agree. However, the committee may continue with the case if they think it is against the public interest to withdraw.

the effect of registering a fair rent

Once a fair rent is registered, this is the maximum rent that the landlord can ask to be paid as from the effective date of the registration. For a rent assessed by a rent officer, the effective date is normally the date of registration; for one that has been determined by a rent assessment committee, it is the date of their decision.

A registration remains in force until a new application for registration is made or until the registration is cancelled. This is so notwithstanding any change of tenant (provided of course that he has a regulated tenancy), or a change of landlord.

If the fair rent is lower than the rent previously paid by the tenant, the landlord must reduce the rent from the effective date. If the tenant has been paying a higher rent than one already registered, however, which sometimes happens when a new tenant is unaware that a fair rent has been registered for the property, he can recover (by adjustment of rent until the overpayment is recovered, or through a county court action) the overpayments made in the past two years. The rent officer is not involved in recovery of rent.

if the fair rent is higher

Where a fair rent is determined by a rent officer and he (or, following an objection, a rent assessment committee) decides to increase the tenant's rent so that the fair rent is greater than that currently being charged, the whole of the increase becomes payable.

However, unless the tenancy is still protected and the

agreement allows for increases, the landlord must serve a prescribed notice of increase (the form for which is available from law stationers) on the tenant before he can claim the increased rent.

If the tenancy is protected and the agreement does not allow for increases, the landlord cannot start charging the fair rent until he has ended the tenancy. (He will probably not be able to do this if the tenancy is for a fixed term, but would have to wait until the term expires.) A periodic tenancy is usually ended by notice to quit; but to save the landlord having to serve both notices, a notice of increase can serve two purposes. Provided it is for the same length as the notice to quit, it ends the protected tenancy and enables the landlord to charge the increased rent.

The only way in which a registered rent may be varied is by applying for a new rent to be registered or for the present one to be cancelled.

applying for registration of a new fair rent
A new application for re-registration cannot be made until two years have elapsed from the date when the registration last took effect, except where

○ a landlord submits an application for re-registration three months before that date (but any new registration will not take effect until the two years are up); or
○ a joint application is made by the landlord and the tenant; or
○ there has been a material change in the condition of the dwelling or the terms of the tenancy (for example, as to the provision of furniture) and the registered rent is no longer a fair rent.

cancellation
The landlord and the tenant can apply jointly to have a registered rent cancelled. The application has to be made on a prescribed form and two years must have elapsed since the effective date of the last registration. The parties must have

agreed a new rent and a copy of their rent agreement (which must comply with the rules) should accompany the application. One term of the agreement must be that the landlord cannot end the tenancy (except for non-payment of rent or breach of any other covenant) within 12 months of the application for cancellation.

The rent officer can only cancel if he is satisfied that the rent payable under the proposed agreement is a fair one and that any terms for variation of payments for services, maintenance and repair are reasonable. There is no right of appeal from his decision. If he decides not to cancel, the registered rent continues in force.

Once the registered rent is cancelled, the parties can make further rent agreements. A cancellation stops neither party from later applying to the rent officer to determine a fair rent.

A landlord may apply for cancellation on his own, if two years have elapsed since the effective date of the last registration and the premises are not currently let to a regulated tenant.

new regulated tenancy after January 1989
In only very limited circumstances can a new regulated tenancy be granted after 15 January 1989; and if there was no fair rent registered in respect of the property during a previous tenancy, the parties can agree on whatever rent they choose. Once they have agreed a figure for rent, that figure can only be increased if the tenancy is still protected and the agreement so provides or, where the agreement does not provide for increases, by formal rent increase. Such an agreement must be in writing, signed by both parties and state in characters not less conspicuous than those used in any other part of the agreement that the tenant's security of tenure under the Rent Act will not be affected if he refuses to enter into the agreement, and that in any event he may apply at any time to the rent officer for a rent to be registered.

premiums and other payments

It is a criminal offence to require or receive a premium or key money as a condition of renewal or continuance of a protected tenancy or for the transfer (assignment) of it to a new tenant. On conviction, the landlord may be ordered to repay the money and is liable to a fine. The payment does not have to be made to the landlord to constitute an illegal premium; it can be made to his agent or to a tenant who is transferring the tenancy.

A premium includes any payment in addition to rent – for example, the excess over a reasonable price for furniture. A landlord may, however, take a deposit from a tenant of furnished or unfurnished premises, provided it is not more than one-sixth of the annual rent and is reasonable in relation to the tenant's potential liability.

It is also an offence to require a tenant to pay rent in advance of the rental period it covers (suppose it is a monthly tenancy, the landlord cannot demand December's rent in November but he can ask for it on 1 December) or to pay rent more than six months in advance. The tenant is entitled to recover any rent so paid.

It is not an offence for the landlord to pay the tenant for the surrender of the lease, although any agreement or contract to this effect will be unenforceable.

special note for existing tenants

Generally, if you are an existing protected or statutory tenant and you give it up to take a new tenancy in the same or other accommodation owned by the same landlord, that tenancy cannot be an assured tenancy under the Housing Act 1988. It can still be a protected tenancy provided it does not fall within one or more of the exceptions to the Rent Act 1977. If you are a protected shorthold tenant, special rules apply. These are explained later in the book.

when the tenant dies

The rules in the Rent Act 1977 which govern who is entitled to succeed to a regulated tenancy have been amended by section 39 and Schedule 4 of the Housing Act 1988 for deaths occurring after 14 January 1989. However, it is still necessary to see how succession worked under the old law, because the new rules depend on the status of the tenant at his death.

death before 15 January 1989

On the death of the original tenant, whether still protected or statutory, the tenancy was automatically transferred as a statutory tenancy to a 'first successor', who could be either

○ the tenant's husband or wife, provided he or she was living in the property immediately before the tenant died; or, if no spouse,

○ any member of the tenant's family who was living with the tenant on a permanent basis during the six months preceding his death. 'Family' was not confined to its traditional meaning of mother, father, in-laws, children, grandchildren, brothers, sisters, uncles and aunts, and so on. It included, for example, a so-called common-law wife or husband. There must however have been a familial link between the tenant and the claimant; platonic relationships did not count, nor non-familial relationships between persons of the same sex. If more than one member of the family qualified, succession could be decided between them by agreement, or, if necessary, by the county court.

When a first successor died, the tenancy could be transmitted as a statutory tenancy to a 'second successor'. A second successor succeeded in exactly the same way as a first, namely the first successor's surviving husband or wife, or, where no surviving spouse, a resident member of the first successor's family. When the second successor died, the statutory tenancy came to an end.

A statutory tenancy by succession operated in exactly the same way as a statutory tenancy which arises on the ending of a protected tenancy.

deaths occurring on or after 15 January 1989

On the death of the original tenant, whether still protected or statutory, the tenancy is automatically transferred as a statutory tenancy to the tenant's spouse, provided he or she was living with the tenant in the property immediately before the tenant died. Spouse includes a so-called common-law husband or wife. If more than one person qualifies as a 'spouse', and succession cannot be decided between them by agreement, the county court can be asked to decide.

If there is no surviving spouse, the first successor will be any member of the tenant's family who was living in the property with the tenant on a permanent basis during the two years preceding his death. (For a transitional period of 18 months after the commencement of the Housing Act, six months residence before 15 January 1989 and continuous residence thereafter will suffice.) Member of the family means the same as under the old rules (but for common-law wife or husband). But the member of the tenant's family does not succeed to a statutory tenancy as before; instead, he becomes entitled to an assured periodic tenancy under the Housing Act 1988. (The terms of this assured periodic tenancy by succession are explained below.)

what happens when a first successor dies?
If the first successor was an assured tenant (that is, a member of an original protected or statutory tenant's family who has succeeded to an assured periodic tenancy on or after 15 January 1989), there is then no further succession. The landlord will be able to get a mandatory court order under ground 7 of the Housing Act 1988 for possession against any surviving spouse or other person who has inherited the tenancy.

If the first successor was a statutory tenant (either because he or she succeeded to the tenancy of an original protected or statutory tenant before 15 January 1989, or because he or she was the spouse of an original protected or statutory tenant who died on or after 15 January 1989), a second succession is allowed. But to qualify, a second successor must have

○ been a member of both the original tenant's family and the family of the first successor; and
○ resided in the property with the first successor during the two years preceding his death.

A second successor becomes entitled to an assured periodic tenancy under the Housing Act 1988.

what happens when a second successor dies?

If the second successor was a statutory tenant (because he succeeded to a first successor's statutory tenancy before 15 January 1989), the statutory tenancy simply comes to an end.

If the second successor was an assured tenant (because he succeeded to a first successor's statutory tenancy on or after 15 January 1989), the landlord has the right to obtain a mandatory court order for possession under ground 7 of the Housing Act 1988, against anyone who has become entitled to the tenancy under the second successor's will or on his intestacy.

terms of an assured tenancy by succession

Where a successor becomes entitled to an assured periodic tenancy under the above rules, the tenancy is one which is deemed to

○ arise immediately on the death of the former protected or statutory tenant; and
○ be granted by the person who was the landlord of the property at the time when the former protected or statutory tenant died; and

○ be of the same accommodation as that formerly let to the deceased tenant; and
○ be for the same period as that for which rent was last payable by the deceased tenant (so, for example, if the deceased tenant last paid rent monthly, the assured tenancy will be a monthly assured periodic tenancy); and
○ be on the same terms as those under which the deceased tenant last occupied the accommodation, insofar as these are consistent with the nature of an assured periodic tenancy by succession; and
○ be a statutory periodic assured tenancy for the purposes of rent levels.

new rent
An assured periodic tenancy by succession is subject to the rent regulation provisions contained in section 13 of the Housing Act 1988. Any provision in the deceased tenant's protected or statutory tenancy which allowed the landlord to increase the rent is not carried forward into the assured periodic tenancy. A landlord can only increase the rent by serving notice on the tenant in accordance with section 13 of the Housing Act 1988, and the tenant can refer an increase to a rent assessment committee for determination. The section 13 procedure is fully explained earlier (page 64 onward).

For the purposes of rent regulation, the assured periodic tenancy by succession is treated as a statutory periodic assured tenancy. Practically, this means that the landlord can serve a section 13 notice to increase the rent the minute the 'minimum period' after the start of the tenancy has expired. In the case of a yearly tenancy, the minimum period is six months; for a tenancy of less than one month, it is one month; and in any other case, it is the period of the tenancy. Thereafter, the landlord can serve notice to increase the rent at yearly intervals, provided he additionally gives the minimum period of notice.

Once a rent has been determined by a rent assessment committee, that is the maximum rent the landlord can charge for a forthcoming period. Any express term for rent (or its determination) in the deceased tenant's tenancy which is inconsistent with this will therefore be of no effect. There is however nothing to stop the new tenant and the landlord together coming to a new agreement.

inconsistent terms

A covenant not to assign the tenancy in whole or in part, or to sub-let, or part with possession of the whole or any part of the accommodation without the consent of the landlord, is implied by section 15 of the Housing Act 1988 into every assured periodic tenancy by succession. A landlord may refuse his consent on reasonable or unreasonable grounds. Any term of the deceased's tenancy providing differently does not apply.

new terms

If the deceased tenant had a fixed term tenancy which had not come to an end, section 6 of the Housing Act 1988 applies to the assured periodic tenancy by succession. Section 6 enables either the landlord or the tenant to serve notice on the other proposing new terms for the tenancy (other than rent) and an adjustment of rent to take account of these new terms; the other may then refer the notice to a rent assessment committee if he is dissatisfied with these terms. The section 6 procedure is fully explained earlier (page 59 onward).

Note that both section 13 and section 6 of the Housing Act 1988 offer wide scope to a landlord to vary the terms of a tenancy. Successor tenants who are not happy with proposed new terms should ensure that they respond quickly to notices.

getting vacant possession

Where the original tenancy was granted under case 11 (returning owner-occupier), case 12 (future retirement home), case 16 (farmworker letting), case 17 (farmhouse letting), case 18 (farm manager letting) or case 20 (letting by serviceman) in Schedule 15 to the Rent Act 1977, these grounds for possession remain available to a landlord against an assured periodic tenant by succession.

Furthermore, any notice given to the original tenant for the purposes of case 13 (out of holiday season letting), case 14 (out of student term letting), or case 15 (clergy letting), counts as the proper notice for the purposes of the corresponding grounds 3, 4 and 5 in Schedule 2 to the Housing Act 1988.

Otherwise, all the grounds for possession set out in Schedule 2 to the Housing Act 1988 are available to a landlord (although mandatory grounds 1(b) (landlord requires property as principal home), and 2 (mortgagee seeking possession) will not apply unless the court dispenses with the prior notice requirement.

It is important, however, to realise that possession actions against assured periodic tenants by succession are brought under the Housing Act 1988, even if on a case under the Rent Act 1977. A landlord must give proper notice of proceedings for possession. The necessary contents and length of the notice are described at pages 56 and 57. For the purposes of length, an assured periodic tenancy by succession is treated the same as any other periodic assured tenancy.

phasing out protected shorthold tenancies

The protected shorthold tenancy was a form of regulated tenancy introduced by the Housing Act 1980. It represented an earlier move to encourage private landlords to let their property rather than sell it. Landlords could create short lets of dwellings which would be free from the normal security of tenure provisions when the term expired, but still within the fair rent system of the Rent Act 1977.

When first introduced, protected shortholds were unpopular with landlords because the compulsory registration of a fair rent was a condition to their grant. Even when this ceased to be a requirement, the protected shorthold enjoyed only limited success, mainly due to the complicated procedure that had to be followed by landlords who wished to exercise their mandatory right to an order for possession at the end of the term.

No protected shorthold tenancies can (with one limited exception) be created after 15 January 1989. The Housing Act 1988 offers landlords the assured shorthold as the equivalent. However, protected shortholds created before 15 January 1989 continue to be governed by the Rent Act 1977. Those which do not disappear through landlords properly obtaining possession will gradually be phased out by the new succession provisions introduced by the Housing Act 1988.

what was a protected shorthold?

Any dwelling that could be let on a normal protected tenancy could be let on a protected shorthold. In other words, any non-resident private landlord could let furnished or unfurnished accommodation on protected shorthold – provided he satisfied certain conditions, such as the tenancy being granted to a new tenant or agreed upon after 28 November 1980 and before 15 January 1989, and for a fixed term of between one and five years which could not be prematurely brought to an end (except by forfeiture if the tenant broke one of the terms of the agreement).

Prior to the grant of the tenancy, the landlord had to give the tenant a notice in the prescribed form; and for all protected shortholds granted before 1 December 1981 and all protected shortholds in Greater London granted before 4 May 1987, either a fair rent had to be registered at the time of the grant of the tenancy or the landlord had to obtain a certificate of fair rent before the grant of the tenancy.

the notice
The prescribed form of shorthold notice informed the tenant that he was being offered a protected shorthold tenancy. If the tenant was an existing protected or statutory tenant, he was warned that if he accepted a protected shorthold of other accommodation he would have less security of tenure. The registered rent (if any) had to be inserted into the notice, and there followed a statement that this was the maximum rent the tenant could be charged. If no fair rent had been registered for the accommodation, the agreed rent had to be filled in. The tenant was then told that either party could apply at any time to the rent officer for the registration of a fair rent.

the rights of the parties during the protected shorthold term

What follows is necessarily only relevant to protected shorthold tenants whose tenancy was granted before 15 January 1989 (or pursuant to a contract made before that date).

ending the tenancy
During the fixed term, the tenant is Rent Act protected as far as security of tenure is concerned. Unless the tenancy agreement provides for forfeiture for non-payment of rent or breach of any of the other terms of the tenancy, the landlord cannot bring the tenancy to a premature end. (If the tenancy agreement contains any other term giving the landlord the right to terminate the tenancy before the end of the fixed term, then the tenancy is, in fact, a fully protected – regulated – one.)

The tenant, on the other hand, has the right to end the tenancy during the fixed term. If the term is for 2 years or less, he must give the landlord one month's notice in writing; if for over 2 years, three months' notice in writing. This right cannot be contracted out of in the tenancy agreement, and any term which purports to impose a penalty or disability on the tenant if he gives notice, cannot be enforced.

assignment and sub-letting

A protected shorthold tenant may not assign (that is transfer his interest in) the tenancy to someone else. He may, however, sub-let the whole or part of his accommodation – provided the agreement permits him to do so. But a sub-letting does not affect the landlord's right to regain possession at the end of the fixed term: if a possession order is obtained against a head protected shorthold tenant, the sub-tenant has to go too (section 137 of the Rent Act 1977 does not apply).

The court has power under the Matrimonial Homes Act 1983 to order the transfer of a protected shorthold tenancy from one spouse to the other, on the granting of divorce or nullity or at any time thereafter.

rent

If a fair rent has been registered in respect of the accommodation, this is the maximum rent the tenant can be charged. Any excess paid by the tenant is recoverable (but only going back two years).

If no fair rent has been registered for the accommodation, the tenant must pay the contractual rent. A landlord may not increase the contractual rent, unless the agreement allows him to do so, or he makes a formal rent agreement with the tenant.

The tenant may at any time apply to the rent officer to have a fair rent registered (although this may be one incentive to a landlord to seek to regain possession at the end of the fixed term).

the rights of the parties at the end of the fixed term

Again, this is only of concern to protected shorthold tenants whose tenancies were granted before 15 January 1989 (or pursuant to a contract made before that date).

Case 19, added to Schedule 15 to the Rent Act 1977 by the Housing Act 1980, gives the landlord a right to possession at the end of the protected shorthold term, provided he follows the correct procedure. This involves him in two stages. First, during the last three months of the protected shorthold term he must give the tenant at least three months' written notice of his intention to apply for a possession order under case 19 (known as the appropriate notice). Second, he must take proceedings in the county court to obtain possession within three months of the expiry of the appropriate notice.

Provided that the landlord fulfilled the conditions for creating a protected shorthold tenancy, has served a valid appropriate notice and taken possession proceedings within the proper time, the court must grant an order for possession against the tenant. If it thinks it just and equitable to do so, the court may grant the landlord a possession order even if he did not fulfil certain of the protected shorthold conditions, namely serving the tenant with a protected shorthold notice before the grant of the tenancy or complying with the compulsory rent registration requirement where applicable.

if the time limits are not observed
If the landlord fails to serve an appropriate notice of his intention to apply for possession under case 19 before the end of the fixed term, or fails to take possession proceedings within the three months time limit, he still retains the right to possession, but he must wait until three months before the anniversary of the fixed term before he can serve his appropriate notice. So if, for example, the protected shorthold term ended on 31 December 1988, but he did not serve his appropriate notice between 1 October and 31 December 1988, he can do so between 1 October and 31 December 1989.

The result, from the tenant's point of view, is that he can remain in possession on a yearly basis. Once the fixed term ends, however, the tenant becomes a statutory tenant, and all the grounds for possession in Schedule 15 to the Rent Act 1977 become available to the landlord; he can offer suitable alternative accommodation, for instance. Such alternative accommodation would normally be let under an assured tenancy. But the wording of the Housing Act 1988 suggests that even where the original tenancy was a protected shorthold, the court may direct during the possession proceedings that the alternative accommodation be let on a protected (regulated) tenancy if it is of the view that an assured tenancy would not offer the tenant the required security. In this event, the new protected tenancy cannot be shorthold because a protected shorthold cannot be granted to someone who was formerly a protected or statutory tenant. It may well be that the court will direct that case 19 should continue to apply to what will otherwise be a normal protected tenancy of the alternative accommodation. It remains to be seen how the courts deal with this problem.

It should be appreciated that a tenant who was originally granted a protected shorthold may have been living in his accommodation for several years as a statutory tenant, his landlord never having availed himself of the proper procedure for obtaining possession.

If, before 15 January 1989, instead of just allowing a protected shorthold tenant to hold over (that is, stay on) at the end of the protected shorthold term, the landlord granted the tenant a new tenancy (at his own, or the tenant's option), this new tenancy could not be a protected shorthold because it was granted to someone who was already a protected or statutory tenant. The new tenancy was an ordinary protected tenancy, but the landlord still retained his right to recover possession under case 19.

If, on or after 15 January 1989, a landlord grants a new tenancy to

– a protected shorthold tenant, or
– a protected or statutory tenant under a tenancy to which case 19 applies,

the new tenancy is an assured shorthold tenancy under the Housing Act 1988 (even though it does not fulfil the assured shorthold conditions), unless, before the start of the tenancy the landlord serves notice on the tenant that it is not to be a shorthold tenancy (in which case it will be an ordinary assured tenancy).

death of tenant before 15 January 1989

The rules which specified who was entitled to succeed to a protected shorthold, or to a protected or statutory tenancy to which case 19 still applied, were the same as for ordinary regulated tenancies. However, the statutory tenancy to which the successor became entitled was subject to case 19, so that the landlord retained his right to regain possession.

death of tenant on or after 15 January 1989

Again, the rules are the same as for ordinary regulated tenancies. However, where a successor becomes entitled to an assured periodic tenancy by succession under those rules, he will get an assured shorthold tenancy. This will happen if the first successor is a member of the deceased tenant's family, or if a second succession is allowed.

phasing out restricted contracts

Certain types of arrangement for residential accommodation called 'restricted contracts' have, since 1974, enjoyed a lesser form of protection under the Rent Act 1977 (as amended by the Housing Act 1980), namely rent control but no security of tenure. Tenancies where there is a resident landlord are the most significant group, but a large number of residential licences are also within the definition of a restricted contract.

No new restricted contracts can be created on or after 15 January 1989 (under section 36 of the Housing Act 1988). But restricted contracts already in existence before that date continue to be governed by the Rent Act 1977.

what is a restricted contract?

The statutory definition of a restricted contract is meagre: "a contract . . . whereby one person grants to another person, in consideration of a rent which includes payment for the use of furniture or for services, the right to occupy a dwelling as a residence" (section 19 Rent Act 1977).

In practice, a restricted contract would have arisen before 15 January 1989 in the following circumstances:

○ where a tenancy was granted by a resident landlord; or
○ where the tenant shared living accommodation with his landlord; or
○ where the rent payable for a tenancy or licence included a payment for services or furniture.

In the first two instances (resident landlord and landlord sharing living accommodation), the requirement for furniture and services did not have to be satisfied.

A restricted contract would not, however, have arisen where:

○ the rateable value of the occupier's part of the premises was more than £1,500 in Greater London and £750 elsewhere;
○ the rent included a substantial payment for board (that is meals);
○ the landlord was the Crown, a government department, local authority, a registered housing association or a housing co-operative;
○ the letting was a protected tenancy with full Rent Act

protection. (The restricted contract net caught those tenancies which were excluded from being protected tenancies because, for instance, the rent included a substantial payment for attendance – cleaning and laundry – or the tenancy was a student let.)

o the contract was to occupy a dwelling for a holiday;
o the occupier (licensee) had no separate accommodation.

the protection

An occupier with a restricted contract that was created before 15 January 1989 continues to be protected by the Rent Act in two ways. First, he cannot be made to leave the premises when the contract comes to an end, unless the landlord obtains an order for possession from the county court. The court may postpone the operation of a possession order for up to three months.

Secondly, the occupier is entitled to refer the contract to a rent tribunal (which is a rent assessment committee in another guise) in order for a 'reasonable rent' to be registered. The procedure and effect is similar to the registration of a fair rent. But a periodic tenant should be warned that if a reasonable rent is registered which is lower than the contractual rent, his landlord may well end the tenancy by serving notice to quit and obtain an order for possession. The tenant can only ask the court to postpone the possession order for three months, so he will not be able to enjoy the benefit of the lower rent for very long.

A reasonable rent tends to be somewhere in between a fair rent and a market rent.

If the rent under an existing restricted contract is varied after 15 January 1989 (other than by a rent tribunal or to accord with a previous registration of a reasonable rent), then the parties are deemed to have entered into a new contract and this cannot be a restricted contract.

a gap in the protection

Tenancies created after 14 January 1989 where there is a resident landlord, or where the tenant shares living accommodation with the landlord, are excluded from being assured tenancies under the Housing Act 1988. Moreover, tenancies or licences created after 14 January 1989 where there is a resident landlord or licensor, or where the tenant or licensee shares living accommodation with the landlord or licensor, are also excluded tenancies and licences under the Protection from Eviction Act 1977.

Most tenancies created after 14 January 1989 where furniture or services are provided will be assured tenancies under the Housing Act 1988. And most licences created on or after 15 January 1989 where furniture or services are provided will fall within the Protection from Eviction Act 1977. (The Protection from Eviction Act 1977 is discussed later, page 246 onward.)

where there is not a resident landlord

The general rule is that if a landlord ceases to be a resident landlord, a restricted contract tenancy becomes a protected tenancy under the Rent Act 1977. (The tenancy itself will necessarily have been created before 15 January 1989.) However, in the following two situations the letting will remain a restricted contract even where the landlord is not resident:

○ If the premises are sold and the buyer (the new landlord) gives the tenant notice within 28 days that he intends to take up residence and does so within 6 months.

○ If a resident landlord has died, two years are allowed for the winding-up of the estate. During this period, a person who has inherited the dwelling may move into residence, or the personal representatives of the deceased landlord may exercise the rights of a resident landlord to obtain possession.

'old-style' assured tenancies

Old-style assured tenancies were introduced by the Housing Act 1980 in order to stimulate the building of new housing for letting in the private sector. Government approved bodies (mainly building societies, pension funds, and property companies) were encouraged to construct new buildings or convert existing ones for residential letting. An old-style assured tenancy was treated as if it were a business tenancy, and Part II of the Landlord and Tenant Act 1954 applied, subject to certain modifications. Very generally, this meant that the tenant had a statutory right to claim a renewal of his lease when it came to an end, and compensation if renewal was refused. The attraction of an old-style assured tenancy from a landlord's point of view was that rents could be fixed at an open market level.

It is no longer possible to create an old-style assured tenancy. All old-style assured tenancies in existence on 15 January 1989 were automatically converted into assured tenancies by section 1(3) Housing Act 1988.

tenancies for mixed residential and business purposes

Lettings of premises which are used for residential and business purposes are excluded from protection under the Housing Act 1988. (They were also excluded from protection under the Rent Act 1977.) Instead, such lettings come under Part II of the Landlord and Tenant Act 1954 (which, like the Housing Act and its predecessor, the Rent Act, applies only to tenancies, not licences). Although the Act defines 'business' widely to mean any trade, profession or employment, within the context of this book, it affects, in the main, shops let with living accommodation above.

Sometimes premises are let for residential purposes and then used by the tenant for his business. Whether such activity constitutes the carrying on of a 'business', for the purposes of the 1954 Act, is a question of degree and would have to be decided in the light of all the circumstances. If the tenant takes in lodgers, for example, the number of rooms, size of the establishment, sums involved and services provided, would all be relevant factors.

The tenant's protection (under Part II of the 1954 Act) is twofold: security of tenure and compensation for displacement. There is no initial rent control.

security of tenure

The tenant is a residential occupier within section 1 of the Protection from Eviction Act 1977 and cannot be evicted without a court order.

After the original agreement ends, the tenancy automatically continues until it is ended by the tenant serving at least four weeks' notice to quit (for a periodic tenancy) or giving three months' notice in writing (if his tenancy was for a fixed term). Or the landlord can serve notice in the prescribed form not less than six months or more than twelve months before the tenancy is to end. If the landlord wishes to obtain possession of the premises and would oppose an application by the tenant for a new tenancy, he must say so in the notice and state the ground of opposition on which he relies (see below). However, the landlord may not really want possession: his reason for serving the notice may merely be to end the old tenancy so that the tenant applies for a new tenancy under which the rent can be brought in line with current market rents.

If the tenant is unwilling to give up possession, he must serve a counter-notice to this effect (there is no prescribed form for this) within two months, and if he cannot agree a new tenancy with his landlord, he must apply to the court for a new tenancy within two to four months after the landlord's notice.

tenant's request
Instead of waiting for the landlord to act, the tenant can himself bring matters to a head by requesting a new tenancy. This right is only available to tenants who were originally granted a fixed term tenancy of more than one year and provided the landlord has not served notice as above.

The tenant's request is made on a prescribed form. If the parties are not agreed as to the grant of a new tenancy, the tenant may apply to the court for one. He must make his application within two to four months of serving his notice requesting a new tenancy. Unless the court gave its approval before the start of the original agreement, it is not possible by agreement to exclude the tenant's right to request a new tenancy.

renewal by the court
The court may grant a periodic or a fixed term tenancy for up to fourteen years. The court has wide discretion to decide the other provisions of the new agreement. The terms of the new lease will largely be governed by the terms of the old lease,

unless either party can show that a variation should be made in the light of accepted commercial practice. If the court has to fix a rent, this will be an open market rent, disregarding such factors as any goodwill attaching to the premises because of the tenant's business there, and any improvements made by the tenant (other than any made because of a contractual obligation to the landlord).

The original tenancy continues until the court hearing and any notice ending it is deferred for at least three months after the final hearing.

grounds for opposition

The landlord can oppose the tenant's application to the court for a new tenancy on any of the grounds specified in section 30 of the Landlord and Tenant Act 1954. These are:

○ disrepair caused by the tenant's failure to carry out his tenancy obligations (only if the disrepair is very bad and the tenant does not remedy the situation before the date of the hearing)
○ persistent delay by the tenant in paying his rent
○ other substantial breaches by the tenant of the tenancy agreement
○ the landlord providing suitable alternative accommodation
○ possession being required of the whole property so that it can be let as a whole unit, where the tenant has a sub-tenancy of part
○ the landlord wishing to occupy the premises himself, or demolish or reconstruct the premises.

compensation for displacement
If the landlord successfully opposes the grant of a new tenancy on any of the last three grounds listed above, compensation is payable when the tenant leaves the premises. The amount is three times the rateable value of the premises. If for the past fourteen years the premises were occupied by the tenant or his

predecessors in the same business, the compensation is doubled.

The parties may agree to exclude the compensation for displacement provisions, but only where the tenant has occupied the premises for the purpose of his business for less than five years.

compensation for improvements
Very generally speaking, an outgoing tenant is entitled to compensation for improvements he has made to the premises, other than those he was obliged to carry out under the terms of his tenancy agreement.

warning

The time limits and procedures laid down in the 1954 Act have to be strictly observed. If any problems arise in connection with a tenancy with mixed residential and business use, legal advice should be obtained.

Department of the Environment's and other publications

The Department of the Environment publishes a series of housing booklets, available from local libraries, housing advice centres and citizens advice bureaux. They include:

No. 2 Right to repair
9 Leasehold reform
12 Wanting to move?
15 Local authority shared ownership
18 Housing defects
19 Assured tenancies (Housing Act 1988)
21 "He wants me out" (harassment)
26 The right and duties of landlords & tenants of houses
28 Right of first refusal

The following are due to be published by July 1989:

22 Letting rooms in your home
24 Notice that you must leave
25 Regulated tenancies
27 Management of flats – the rights and duties of landlords and tenants
29 A guide for the tenants of housing associations.

Shelter's *Guide to the Housing Act 1988* (£4.50) is available from 88 Old Street, London EC1V 9HU.

Guide to housing benefit and community charge benefit (£6.50) is a joint publication by the Institute of Housing and SHAC, 189a Old Brompton Road, London SW5 0AR.

LONG LEASES AND THE RIGHT TO STAY ON OR TO ACQUIRE THE FREEHOLD

During the nineteenth century, many leases for 99 or 125 years were created, and these tenancies came to an end in the second half of this century. As regards security of tenure, tenants who occupy living accommodation under long leases (such as for 99 years) are in no better position at common law than periodic tenants when the contractual term comes to an end. Also, generally speaking, long tenancies were granted at such low rents that they did not fall within the security of tenure provisions of the Rent Acts. Part I of the Landlord and Tenant Act 1954 was introduced with a view to providing a measure of security of tenure for long leaseholders who did not fall within the scope of the Rent Acts.

The statutory scheme of protection which gives long term security of tenure is not the only technique for protecting the residential security of tenants. The law may confer on the tenant the right to purchase the freehold reversion from the landlord – thereby enabling the tenant to convert his status from leaseholder to freeholder. (For an account of the 'right to buy' which has become an important feature of the law relating to council tenants see page 185 onward.) Tenants who occupy a house (rather than a flat) under a long lease were given the right to enfranchise (that is, buy the freehold) by the Leasehold Reform Act 1967. The recent Landlord and Tenant Act 1987 has – in certain limited circumstances – conferred on tenants of flats the right collectively to acquire the freehold of the building in which their flats are situated.

security of tenure for long leaseholders

The fact that a tenancy is for a long fixed term (such as fifty years) does not automatically mean that it is not within the protection of the Rent Act 1977 or the Housing Act 1988. However, these two Acts do not apply where the annual rent is less than two-thirds of the property's rateable value, which is the case in most long leases. Where a long tenancy does not fall within the protection of the Rent Act 1977 or the Housing Act 1988, the tenant will, on satisfying certain conditions, have security of tenure under Part I of the Landlord and Tenant Act 1954.

conditions

A tenancy will fall within the protective ambit of Part I of the Landlord and Tenant Act 1954 if the following conditions are satisfied:
- the contractual term of the tenancy was for more than twenty-one years
- the annual rent is less than two-thirds of the rateable value
- the tenant would be protected by the Rent Act 1977, but for the fact that the rent is less than two-thirds of the rateable value.

Also, the premises must have been let as a separate dwelling, and the tenant must occupy those premises (or part of them) as his home.

If the tenant continues to occupy the premises at the end of the term, the tenancy continues indefinitely on the same conditions (because it is automatically continued by statute).

ending the tenancy

During the fixed term, the landlord can only regain possession if the lease contains a forfeiture clause (which is usual) and the tenant is in breach of one of the obligations under the lease.

Unless the lease contains a break clause entitling the tenant to bring the tenancy to an end prematurely, the tenant can only terminate the fixed term tenancy by agreement with the landlord.

After the fixed term has come to an end, either the tenant or the landlord may wish to end the tenancy. (As noted above, unless steps are taken by one of the parties, the original tenancy continues.)

termination by the landlord

If the landlord wishes to recover possession on or after the expiry of the original term he must serve a notice to resume possession. This must give the tenant at least six months', but not more than twelve months' notice.

The notice should inform the tenant that if he is unwilling to give up possession, the landlord will apply to the court for possession on stated grounds. The grounds on which the landlord may recover possession are specified in Schedule 3 to the 1954 Act. They are as follows:

o the tenant has not paid the rent, or has broken some other term of the tenancy
o the tenant or a person living with him has caused a nuisance or annoyance to neighbours, or has been convicted of using the premises for illegal or immoral purposes
o the landlord requires the premises for his own occupation, or for a member of his family
o the landlord has offered suitable alternative accommodation.

These grounds are discretionary: the court may grant an order for possession if it thinks it is reasonable to do so. If the court chooses not to order possession, the tenancy continues on the same terms.

conversion to a statutory tenancy

After the contractual period has ended the landlord may not wish to resume possession, but he may not want the tenancy to continue on the original terms. Instead of serving a notice to resume possession, the landlord may serve a notice proposing a statutory tenancy. (As with a notice to resume possession, the tenant must be given at least six months', but not more than twelve months' notice.) The notice should propose the terms of the statutory tenancy.

Where the landlord proposes a statutory tenancy, the terms should be agreed by the parties two months before the expiry of the notice. If agreement cannot be reached, the parties should apply to the court for resolution of the dispute. (Where the parties cannot agree a new rent, this question cannot be referred to the court, and the rent stipulated in the original lease will continue to be payable. However, once the statutory tenancy has come into existence either party may apply to have a fair rent registered.) In principle, if the terms are not agreed by the parties or an application has not been made to the court at least two months before the expiry of the notice, the notice lapses – in which case the tenancy continues according to its original terms. (This will not be in the land-lord's interest since the rent will continue to be the ground rent which was payable under the original lease.)

If the terms are agreed by the parties or determined by the court, on the expiry of the landlord's notice proposing a statutory tenancy, the tenant becomes a statutory tenant under the Rent Act 1977. Once a statutory tenancy has come into existence the landlord can only recover possession under the provisions of the Rent Act 1977.

termination by the tenant
Where the tenancy is converted into a statutory tenancy after the contractual fixed term has expired, the tenant who wishes to terminate the statutory tenancy is required to comply with the Rent Act 1977. On the assumption that the original contrac-tual tenancy made no provision for premature termination by the tenant, the tenant must give three months' notice to quit.

If the tenant wishes to terminate the tenancy at the end of the original term, he can give one month's notice, and this period of notice may end on the date when the original contractual term expires. Similarly, one month's notice suffices in situations where the parties have allowed the tenancy to continue after the contractual term (without converting it into a statutory tenancy).

proposed change in the law

There is currently before Parliament the Local Government and Housing Bill. It is likely that it will receive the royal assent during the summer of 1989.

The Bill proposes a number of important changes, in particular with regard to security of tenure of long leaseholders.

At present, the security of tenure of tenants occupying residential premises under a long lease at a low rent is governed by Part I of the Landlord and Tenant Act 1954. When a long tenancy expires the landlord may

o allow the contractual tenancy to continue, or
o seek to resume possession on one of a number of stipulated grounds, or
o propose that the tenant should become a statutory tenant (protected by the Rent Act 1977).

The Local Government and Housing Bill introduces a new scheme of protection for long leaseholders at a low rent. Under this scheme, the landlord will be able to propose that the tenant becomes an assured tenant under the Housing Act 1988.

the Leasehold Reform Act 1967 (rented houses)

The Leasehold Reform Act 1967, as amended by subsequent legislation, gives valuable rights to tenants in the private and public sectors who are occupying a house under a long lease at a low rent (commonly called a ground rent). The leases were often 'building' leases at a very low ground rent for terms of 99 or 125 years. Under this type of lease, the tenant built and maintained a house which at the end of the term became the landlord's entitlement. The social problems became considerable after the second world war when many such leases expired.

The purpose of the Leasehold Reform Act 1967 was to allow the tenant

○ to buy the freehold (the tenant's right to enfranchise), or
○ to extend the period of the lease for 50 years, or
○ to remain in occupation of the property when the lease expires.

conditions

For the tenant to be able to exercise the rights created by the legislation, the following conditions must be satisfied:

○ the tenant must be an individual
○ he must have a lease of a house
○ he must have occupied the house as his only or main residence for the whole of the last three years, or for a total of three out of the last ten years
○ the lease must be for a long term
○ the rent must be a low rent
○ the rateable value of the house must fall within prescribed limits.

A tenant who wishes to exercise his right to buy the freehold or to extend the lease must give the landlord notice of this intention either during the original term granted by the lease, or while the contractual tenancy is continuing under Part I of the Landlord and Tenant Act 1954. The landlord has two months in which to serve a counter-notice in which he either admits or opposes the tenant's claim.

must be an individual

In a number of contexts, the law provides security of tenure for individuals but not for corporate tenants. Under the 1967 Act, a company cannot take advantage of the rights to enfranchise or extend the lease.

must be a house

Most detached, semi-detached and terraced houses fall within the requirements of the legislation; flats and maisonettes are excluded. Tenants of flats held on long leases at a low rent have to rely on Part I of the Landlord and Tenant Act 1954 (see above) or the Landlord and Tenant Act 1987 (see below).

However, the tenant of a whole building may have the right to enfranchise even though the building is divided horizontally into maisonettes or flats. If the tenant of a large house divides it into flats, sub-lets the upper floors and lives in the ground floor flat himself, he will be able to buy the freehold or extend the lease of the house, although the sub-tenants cannot.

Problems may occur when premises are used for mixed residential and business purposes. But, as long as such premises can reasonably be called a house, they will come under the Leasehold Reform Act 1967, provided they satisfy the other conditions.

three years' occupation

If a tenant occupies a house for two years by virtue of a monthly tenancy and then takes a long lease of the house at a low rent, the first two years of occupation cannot be used to fulfil the three-year condition: the tenant must wait until three years have elapsed from the date he took the long lease.

The tenant need not live in the whole of the house. He still comes within the legislation if he sub-lets part, provided he has occupied that, or some other part, as his only or main residence for the whole of the last three years or a total of three years during the last ten.

a long lease

A long lease must normally be one which has been granted for a term of more than twenty-one years. However, a lease for less than twenty-one years acquired under the 'right to buy' provisions contained in the Housing Act 1985 is treated as a long lease for these purposes. The tenant does not have to be the original tenant; he may be an assignee (that is, someone who has bought the lease).

a low rent

In general, the annual rent must be less than two-thirds of the rateable value of the house assessed on a particular date, namely whichever is the later of:

○ 23 March 1965
○ the date on which the property first appeared in the valuation list
○ the first day of the term granted by the lease.

A lease will be outside the scope of the 1967 Act if it was granted between 31 August 1939 and 1 April 1963 and the rent at the beginning of the tenancy was more than two-thirds of the letting value of the property. The letting value of a property is the amount which could be obtained by a landlord letting on the open market.

Any amounts paid by a tenant towards the landlord's costs of insuring the building, providing services or carrying out repairs are to be disregarded in calculating the rent, irrespective of when the lease was created.

Rent payable under a shared ownership lease acquired under the Housing Act 1985 is not a low rent for these purposes if it is in excess of £10 a year. (Shared ownership leases are discussed at page 200 onward.)

rateable values

In order for the tenant to have the right to enfranchise or extend his lease, the house which he occupies must fall below a prescribed rateable value. The relevant rateable value depends on the location of the house (whether in Greater London or elsewhere), the date on which the tenancy was created, and the moment when the house first appeared in the valuation list. The relevant rateable value will be a figure between £200 and £1500, depending on the circumstances.

the right to buy the freehold: what can the tenant buy?

A tenant has the right to buy only that which was the subject-matter of a lease. For example, he cannot compel the landlord to sell him a garden, garage or outbuilding which he has been using, unless it was also included in the lease of the house. Similarly, the tenant does not have a right to buy a garage or garden let to him under a totally different lease. It is perfectly permissible, however, for the tenant to agree to buy these, separately, from a landlord. (They will probably be of little use to the landlord or to anyone else.)

Where the landlord retains part of a building the majority of which is occupied by the tenant (such as where the landlord has the use of one small room in a building, the rest of which is the tenant's house), the landlord may, within two months of receiving notice that the tenant wishes to enfranchise, serve a notice on the tenant asking him to buy the whole building. This is to avoid hardship to the landlord who might otherwise be left with something which is valueless. If the tenant refuses to comply with the landlord's request, the matter will ultimately have to be referred to the county court to decide whether it is reasonable for the tenant to buy the part of the building specified in the landlord's notice. A similar procedure exists when a landlord wishes to reduce the extent of the premises he is statutorily bound to sell to the tenant. Again, if the landlord and tenant cannot agree about the reduction, the matter can be referred to the county court, which will have regard to any hardship which would be caused to either party.

Legal ownership of a house does not merely mean owning

bricks and mortar. It includes a bundle of legal rights necessary for the proper enjoyment of the house (for example the right to use pipes and cables crossing a neighbour's land for the supply of electricity, water and other services, or to use a private road running along the back of a house). A tenant will normally be expressly granted such rights in his lease.

The law ensures that when the tenant buys the freehold, he will enjoy similar rights. As far as possible, the landlord must grant to his enfranchising tenant such rights as are necessary to ensure that the latter's position is the same as when he was a tenant.

The law also ensures that the landlord and neighbours retain any rights that they enjoyed before the tenant enfranchised. When the landlord sells the freehold interest in the house, he may insist on retaining some rights which he (or some other person) enjoyed over part of the enfranchising tenant's house when it was held under the long lease.

the right to buy the freehold: the price

The policy of the law is to allow the tenant to buy the freehold at a favourable price. This is achieved by treating the tenant as the owner of the building and the landlord merely as the owner of the land on which the house stands.

The precise mechanism for determining the price to be paid is complex and depends on various assumptions which are stipulated in the 1967 Act (such as that the landlord is willing to sell but the tenant does not have the right to compel him to sell, or that the value of the house has not been increased by any improvements made by the tenant).

disputes as to the price

A landlord or a tenant may ask the local leasehold valuation tribunal (the address is the same as for the rent assessment committee and can be found in the telephone directory) to determine the price to be paid by the tenant who wishes to buy the freehold. Either party may appeal (within 28 days) to the lands tribunal against a decision by the leasehold valuation tribunal. The procedure is very complicated and anyone intending to use it should seek professional advice.

covenants where a tenant enfranchises

A lease usually contains a variety of covenants which impose obligations on both the landlord and the tenant in relation to issues such as the payment of rent and rates, insurance, repairs and use of the property. When a tenant enfranchises and becomes the freehold owner, most of the covenants become inappropriate and therefore disappear. However, the tenant will be bound by interests (such as rights of way and restrictive covenants) which were already attached to the freehold, and will remain bound by sub-tenancies, mortgages etc. created out of his own tenancy.

The Leasehold Reform Act 1967 also provides that in some circumstances the conveyance of the freehold to the tenant may be subject to further obligations:

○ where an estate is controlled by a single landlord, the landlord can apply to the High Court to have a 'scheme of management' approved, which means that, even after a tenant has enfranchised, the landlord will retain certain powers (such as powers to carry out work for maintenance or repair, to regulate development, to require a tenant who has enfranchised to contribute to the maintenance and repair)

○ where the tenant is enfranchising from certain public sector landlords (such as local authorities, new town development corporations etc.), covenants may be imposed on the tenant restricting the carrying out of development or clearing of land where this is necessary to preserve the land for possible development by the original landlord

○ in some cases, where the freehold is acquired from particular landlords (such as the Commission for the New Towns), the landlord may insert in the conveyance to the enfranchising tenant a term that the house should not be resold without the landlord's consent and that the landlord shall have the right to buy back the property in the event of any proposal to sell it.

mortgages

In many cases, the landlord will have mortgaged the freehold perhaps to enable him to buy it in the first place. When the enfranchising tenant acquires the freehold, in order to take the property free from the mortgage, he must pay the purchase price to the mortgagee rather than to the freehold owner. If there is more than one mortgage to be paid off, they must be paid off in order of priority (broadly speaking according to the date on which they were created). If the tenant cannot ascertain whether the landlord has mortgaged his interest, or discover the identity of a mortgagee, he should pay the purchase price into court. The same is true if a mortgagee proves to be unhelpful and, for example, refuses to sign a release of the house from the mortgage.

the right to extend the lease

A tenant who cannot afford to buy the freehold or does not wish to do so, may choose to claim an extension of his existing lease. Once a tenant gives notice to his landlord that he wishes to claim an extension, the landlord has to grant him a new tenancy which will come into effect when the existing one expires. The terms of the new lease will be as follows.

duration
The landlord has to grant an extension of fifty years.

property included in the lease
Broadly speaking, the premises covered by the new lease will

be the same as those contained in the tenant's original lease. However, the landlord may be able to increase or reduce the premises to be included in the new lease, in the same way that he can when the tenant acquires the freehold.

rent

The tenant continues to pay the agreed rent until the date on which his existing lease expires. Thereafter, he has to pay a new ground rent, based on the letting value of the land on which the house stands (ignoring any value attributable to the house or other buildings). The use to which the land may be put will be taken into consideration. So, if the site is suitable for development, the rent will reflect this and be higher. (The landlord can also require the new ground rent to be reviewed after twenty-five years.)

The leasehold valuation tribunal (established by the Housing Act l980 as a forum for disputes about rent, value of freehold, etc) has the power to fix a new ground rent, on the application of either the landlord or the tenant.

Any payment towards services which the landlord has to provide under the terms of the new tenancy will be in addition to the new ground rent. If the tenant's existing lease requires him to contribute a fixed sum towards services and over the course of time this figure has become unrealistic, the legislation provides that 'such provision as may be just' should be made for payments by the tenant. Failing agreement between the parties, the leasehold valuation tribunal may be asked to fix a figure.

other terms

As a general rule, the provisions of the new lease will be the same as those in the tenant's existing lease, although they can be varied by agreement. However, there are some important exceptions to this general rule – for example, it is not possible to include in the new lease a right of renewal of the lease; the new lease will not contain a provision which allows the landlord to terminate the new tenancy otherwise than in the event of breach of covenant by the tenant; the new lease must provide that the landlord has the right to resume possession of the property for the purposes of redeveloping it.

relationship between the right to buy the freehold and the right to extend the lease

When a tenant claims an extension of his lease under the 1967 Act, he retains his right to buy the freehold, but only until the date on which his original lease expires. So, if he does not serve his landlord with notice of his intention to buy the freehold before that date, he will have to give up possession at the end of his extended fifty year lease. He has no right to a further extension under the Act and he will not be protected by the Rent Act 1977 or the Housing Act 1988 when the extended lease expires.

A tenant should remember that his lease will almost certainly contain a covenant by him to repair the property. At the end of his lease he will be required to ensure that the property is in a good state of repair. The landlord may serve a schedule of dilapidations setting out the work he feels necessary to put the premises in proper order. If a tenant has failed to meet his repairing obligations during the tenancy, he may have to pay for his repairs in one lump sum.

the tenant's right to stay on

A tenant may choose not to exercise his right to buy the freehold or claim an extended lease, or perhaps he will not have occupied the property for the qualifying period of three years before the long lease expires. In these circumstances (assuming that the tenancy did not become a protected tenancy during the contractual term), the tenant's right to remain in possession of the property will be governed by Part I of the Landlord and Tenant Act 1954.

opposing a tenant's claim to enfranchise or to an extension

If the conditions laid down by the 1967 Act are not satisfied, the tenant cannot claim any of the rights conferred by it. However, even where the conditions of the legislation are satisfied, a landlord may oppose a claim by his tenant to buy the freehold or extend the lease on one of four grounds.

1.   *landlord requires the property for his own occupation*
The landlord may apply to the county court for possession of the house when the original lease expires. He must apply during the term of the original lease but after the tenant has served notice claiming his rights under the 1967 Act. To oppose the tenant's claim successfully, the landlord must show

○ that he acquired his interest in the house before 19 February 1966
○ that the house or part of it is, or will be, reasonably required by him, or an adult (over 18) member of his family, as his or their only or main residence on the date the tenant's original lease expires
○ that it would cause greater hardship to him or the member of the family if the court did not make an order for possession than would be the case if the tenant had to give up possession at the end of the lease.

The court has discretion as to the granting of such orders. If the landlord is successful, the court will make an order specifying a date when he can re-take possession. The tenant will be entitled to compensation for his loss of the house and premises, the amount of which is assessed as if the landlord had recovered possession for the purposes of redevelopment.

A landlord who makes an unsuccessful application to the court on this ground may submit another application if his circumstances change.

2. *redevelopment*

A landlord whose tenant has claimed an extended lease may regain possession if he intends to demolish or reconstruct the whole or a substantial part of the premises for the purposes of redevelopment. Compensation is payable to the outgoing tenant. (Special provisions apply to landlords which are public authorities.)

3. *where the Crown has an interest*

Generally speaking, the Crown is not bound by the provisions of the Act and the tenant may find that he is unable to take advantage of the 1967 Act. In practice, however, the Crown usually allows a tenant to exercise his right to enfranchise or extend his lease, unless the property is of special architectural or historic interest or is needed for development or some public purpose.

4. *tenant has previously given a notice to quit*

If the landlord can prove that a tenant's notice claiming to acquire the freehold or to extend the lease is made after the tenant has given notice to quit, the claim is invalid.

special provisions relating to sub-tenants

The fact that the tenant in occupation is a sub-tenant does not prevent him from buying the freehold, claiming an extended lease, or staying after the expiry of the contractual term, provided that all the conditions for the application of the 1967 Act are otherwise fulfilled. The law makes special provision to enable all the superior interests (that is, the interest of the landlord of the tenant in occupation and other interests higher up the chain) to be dealt with.

the Landlord and Tenant Act 1987 (rented flats)

One of the problems which has plagued the private rented sector in recent years has been the fact that much rented accommodation has fallen into serious disrepair. The position of tenants of flats and maisonettes is in some ways unsatisfactory since they may find it difficult to force the landlord to do the necessary repairs. The acquisition of the freehold by the tenant (at a significant discount) provides the tenant with an opportunity of taking total responsibility for the premises. The Leasehold Reform Act 1967, however, applies only to tenants of houses, and not to tenants of flats.

The Landlord and Tenant Act 1987 has introduced a number of mechanisms aimed at facilitating the maintenance of rented accommodation. Among these mechanisms are the right of first refusal whereby tenants may acquire the landlord's freehold when he proposes to sell it, and the right of compulsory acquisition.

the right of first refusal

The right of first refusal is established by Part I of the Landlord and Tenant Act 1987. To determine whether the right arises, four elements must be considered: the premises, the landlord, the tenant, and the proposed disposal.

i the premises

In order for premises to fall within the scope of Part I of the Landlord and Tenant Act 1987, the building must be divided into at least two flats, and more than half the number of the flats in the building must be occupied by 'qualifying tenants'. So, the Act will not apply if the building is divided into ten flats and only five are occupied by qualifying tenants.

Premises are also excluded from the scope of this law if more than 50% of the floor area of the building is used for non-residential purposes.

ii the landlord

The landlord for the purposes of Part I of the 1987 Act is the person who is the immediate landlord of the qualifying tenant or, where the premises are occupied by a statutory tenant, the person who would be entitled to possession but for the statutory tenancy.

There are, however, two categories of landlord which are excluded:

○ certain public or quasi-public landlords (including local authorities, Commission for the New Towns, urban development corporations, the Development Board for Rural Wales, the Housing Corporation, housing trusts, housing action trusts established under Part III of the Housing Act 1988 and certain housing associations)
○ landlords who are defined as resident landlords for the purposes of the 1987 Act. A landlord will be a resident landlord if he lives in part of the building which is occupied by the qualifying tenants as long as
  – the building is not a purpose-built block of flats
  – the landlord occupies a flat in the premises as his only or principal home
  – he has occupied the flat for at least twelve months.

iii the tenant

A tenant will be a 'qualifying' tenant within the meaning of Part I of the 1987 Act unless his tenancy falls within one of the following categories:

○ protected shorthold tenancy
○ a business tenancy under Part II of the Landlord and Tenant Act 1954
○ a tenancy terminable on the cessation of employment
○ an assured tenancy.

In principle, there is no requirement that the tenant should have a long lease in order to be a qualifying tenant. However, the fact that assured tenants under the Housing Act 1988 are excluded means that, in relation to premises which are let after

15 January 1989, most periodic tenants and tenants under short fixed terms will not be qualifying tenants. Long leases, on the other hand, will not normally be assured tenancies since the annual rent will be less than two-thirds of the rateable value. Accordingly, a tenant who occupies premises by virtue of a long lease granted after the Housing Act 1988 came into force will normally be a qualifying tenant for the purposes of the Landlord and Tenant Act 1987.

iv the proposed disposal

A relevant disposal will occur if

○ the transaction proposed by the landlord involves the disposal of any estate (or interest) in the premises, and
○ the proposed transaction is not excluded.

The most important categories of the excluded transactions are the following:

○ the grant of a tenancy of a single flat
○ the grant of a secured interest (such as a mortgage). However, where the landlord's reversion (the freehold) has been mortgaged, a disposal by the mortgagee in the exercise of a power of sale constitutes a relevant disposal (although the grant of a mortgage is exempt)
○ disposal to a trustee in bankruptcy or to the liquidator of a company
○ transfers ordered by the court in the context of matrimonial or succession proceedings
○ disposal following a compulsory purchase order
○ a gift to a member of the landlord's family or to a charity
○ the surrender of a lease (where the lease makes provision for such a surrender to take place)
○ disposal to the Crown
○ disposal by a corporate landlord to an associated company.

where the four conditions are satisfied

In situations where the right of first refusal arises, the landlord must serve a notice on the qualifying tenants setting out the terms of the disposal, including a statement of the property which he proposes to sell and the price. The notice must

○ state that it constitutes an offer by the landlord to dispose of the property on those terms which may be accepted by the requisite majority of the qualifying tenants

○ specify a period in which the offer must be accepted (not less than two months).

Where the landlord has not served a notice on all the qualifying tenants he will nevertheless have complied with his obligation under the Act if, assuming that there are fewer than ten qualifying tenants, he has served the notice on all but one of them, or where there are ten or more qualifying tenants he has served the notice on at least 90% of them.

The tenants' response to the notice is of crucial importance. The tenants should have a meeting to decide whether or not to acquire the landlord's interest. The right of first refusal will lapse unless the landlord's offer is accepted by the requisite majority (more than 50%) of the qualifying tenants (one flat, one vote).

The requirement of a majority of more than 50% means that where there are only two qualifying tenants, both will have to vote in favour of exercising the right of first refusal. Where there are ten qualifying tenants, at least six will have to vote in favour.

If a majority vote in favour of acquiring the freehold, the tenants are given a further two months in which to nominate the person or persons who will purchase the landlord's interest on the tenants' behalf. One possibility is for a tenants' association to nominate itself as purchaser.

If, in the two months period, the tenants do not make the necessary nomination, in the next twelve months the landlord can go ahead with the proposed transaction – that is, sell the freehold to someone else – as long as the price is at least as high as that contained in the notice sent out to the qualifying tenants. If, however, the tenants do nominate within the two months, they then have a further three months in which to complete the purchase. The tenants do not incur any liability to the landlord if they pull out during this three months period.

If the tenants fail to complete the purchase by the end of the three months period, the landlord may – at any point during the next twelve months – sell the premises to any willing purchaser. Again, the price must not be lower than that contained in the original notice.

failure to comply with the procedure

If the landlord sells his interest without complying with the 1987 Act (for example, he sells without serving the original notice on the qualifying tenants) the tenants have a right to acquire the freehold from the purchaser.

This right can be enforced against the purchaser if a majority of the qualifying tenants serve a notice on the new landlord within two months of their being informed that the disposal has taken place. (This should normally occur when the notices required by section 3 of the Landlord and Tenant Act 1985 are served; see page 242 onward.)

If the new landlord re-sells the property, the qualifying tenants can enforce their right to acquire the freehold against the subsequent purchaser.

To avoid these problems, if a prospective purchaser of the freehold is worried that the disposal might be caught by the 1987 Act, he may take action to ensure that the tenants will not subsequently be able to claim the right to acquire the freehold:

○ he should serve a notice on at least 80% of the tenants who occupy the flats in the property which he proposes to buy

○ the notice should inform the tenants of the principal terms of the proposed disposal, and ask the tenants whether the current landlord has served a notice as required by the Act, or – if the landlord has not served such a notice – whether the tenants would wish to exercise the right of first refusal.

The purchaser may go ahead with the sale free from the danger of the tenants exercising the right to acquire the freehold against him if:

○ within the twenty-eight days following the service of the notice by the prospective purchaser not more than 50% of the tenants have replied to the prospective purchaser's notice, or
○ more than 50% of the tenants reply to the notice stating either that they were not entitled to have a notice served on them by the landlord or that they would not wish to exercise the right of first refusal.

the right of compulsory acquisition

The right of first refusal is not a right of compulsory acqui-sition, since the landlord cannot be required to sell to the tenants if he does not wish to sell the premises at all. In this sense, the right of first refusal is very different from the right to acquire the freehold which is created by the Leasehold Reform Act 1967.

In addition to the creation of the right of first refusal, Part III of the Landlord and Tenant Act 1987 establishes for tenants of flats a right of compulsory acquisition. The way in which this right can be exercised is by the tenants' applying to the court for an 'acquisition order'. The conditions which have to be satisfied before the court would make an acquisition order are very stringent.

Four matters must be considered.

i   statutory criteria

The tenants will not be entitled to acquire the freehold under Part III of the 1987 Act unless the following criteria are satisfied.

First, the court must be satisfied that the landlord is in breach of his management obligations and that the breach is likely to continue and the appointment of a manager would not be an adequate remedy, or it must be shown that a manager has been appointed and that he has been managing the property throughout the previous three years.

Secondly, the court can only make an acquisition order if it considers it appropriate to make the order in the circumstances of the case.

ii   qualifying tenants

The right of compulsory purchase can only be exercised by qualifying tenants. The definition of a qualifying tenant under Part III is different from that which applies to Part I. Subject to the exception outlined below, a person is a qualifying tenant if:

○ he occupies a flat by virtue of a long lease (which for the 1987 Act means a lease for a term exceeding twenty-one years) and

○ the tenancy is not protected under Part II of the Landlord and Tenant Act 1954.

The 1987 Act excludes from the category of qualifying tenants a person who would otherwise be a qualifying tenant but who, by virtue of one or more long leases none of which are covered by Part II of the Landlord and Tenant Act 1954, is also the tenant of at least two other flats in the premises.

iii   the premises

Generally, premises will fall within the scope of the right of compulsory acquisition if:

○ they consist of the whole or part of a building

○ they contain two or more flats held by qualifying tenants of the landlord
○ where the premises contain fewer than four flats, all of the flats are let by the landlord on long leases
○ where the premises contain more than three and fewer than ten flats they are all, or all but one, let on long leases.
○ where the premises contain ten or more flats, at least 90% of the flats are let on long leases.

However, premises will be excluded if:

○ more than 50% of the total internal floor area of the premises is occupied or intended to be occupied for other than residential purposes.

Similarly, the premises will be excluded if the landlord is an exempt or resident landlord or the premises are included within the functional land of a charity.

iv   the procedure

The qualifying tenants must serve a preliminary notice. This notice should state that the tenants intend to make an application for an acquisition order. Since the rationale of an acquisition order is that the landlord is in breach of his management obligations, the notice must indicate the tenants' complaint, and the landlord must be given a reasonable amount of time to remedy the breach complained of (if capable of remedy). The court may dispense with the requirement of notice if it is satisfied that it would not be reasonably practicable to serve a notice on the landlord.

After the period specified in the notice has elapsed (or if the court dispenses with the requirement of a notice), the qualifying tenants may apply to the court for an acquisition order. The application must be made by a majority (that is, more than 50%) of the qualifying tenants. As with the right of first refusal, the tenants must nominate the person or persons who are to acquire the freehold on their behalf.

As long as the statutory criteria are satisfied, the court will make the order vesting the freehold in the nominated person or persons. The terms of the order (such as the purchase price) may be agreed between the parties. In default of agreement, the issue should be referred to the rent assessment committee which has jurisdiction to determine the terms on which the landlord's interest may be acquired by the nominated person.

PUBLIC SECTOR TENANCIES

The Rent Act 1977 and the Housing Act 1988 apply only to tenants who rent their homes from private sector landlords (individuals, companies and other organisations which are not designated as public landlords). Until very recently, tenants in the public sector (council tenants and tenants of certain designated public or quasi-public bodies) did not come within any statutory scheme conferring security of tenure. The assumption was that it was safe and proper to give to local authority landlords a complete discretion with regard to the eviction of public sector tenants, and to rely on them to exercise such discretion fairly and wisely.

The Housing Act 1980 introduced a scheme of security of tenure for public sector tenants which was in many ways similar to that which operated in the private sector. Although one of the most important aspects of the scheme established by the 1980 Act was the introduction of security of tenure, council tenants have numerous other statutory rights, including the right to take lodgers and to sublet (with the landlord's consent), the right to carry out repairs, and the right to be given information about the landlord's obligations under the tenancy.

In addition to providing security of tenure, the Housing Act 1980 conferred on most, though not all, council tenants the right to buy. This right entitles a tenant to purchase the landlord's reversion – normally the freehold interest, but sometimes a long leasehold interest. Since 1980, a significant number of council tenants have exercised the right to buy, thereby taking public housing stock out of the public sector into the private owner-occupied sector.

The statutory rights of public sector tenants are now to be found in Part IV of the Housing Act 1985. This Act consolidates the provisions contained in the Housing Act 1980, the Housing and Building Control Act 1984 and the Housing Defects Act 1984. The 1985 Act has since been amended by the Housing and Planning Act 1986 and the Housing Act 1988.

secure tenancy

The key concept in Part IV of the Housing Act 1985 is that of the 'secure tenancy'. It is by virtue of being a secure tenant that an occupier is entitled to the rights contained in the 1985 Act.

The basic requirements of a secure tenancy are as follows:

○ the premises must be a dwelling-house
○ the landlord must be designated
○ the occupier must satisfy certain conditions
○ the arrangement must not fall within one of a number of exclusions.

These points will now be considered in greater detail.

dwelling-house

A secure tenancy can only arise in relation to a dwelling-house. So, a secure tenancy is not created where a local authority grants a tenancy of business premises. Within the context of the Housing Act 1985, a flat, a house or part of a house which is occupied as a residence will generally qualify as a dwelling-house. In addition to the premises being occupied as a residence, they must have been let as a dwelling-house. If premises which are let for business purposes are subsequently used by the tenant exclusively for residential purposes the tenancy does not become a secure tenancy.

the landlord

For tenancies created before 15 January 1989 the landlord must have been one of the following bodies:

○ a local authority, which includes a county, district or London borough council, the Common Council of the City of London or the Council of the Isles of Scilly

○ a new town corporation (which includes both the Commission for the New Towns and development corporations established by an order made, or having effect as if made, under the New Towns Act 1981)

○ an urban development corporation (established under the Local Government, Planning and Land Act 1980)

○ the Development Board for Rural Wales

○ a housing co-operative (approved by the Secretary of State as suitable to exercise the powers of the local housing authority)

○ the Housing Corporation (Maple House, 149 Tottenham Court Road, London W1P 0BN, telephone 01-387 9466)

○ a housing trust which is a charity (the Charity Commissioners, telephone 01-214 6000, keep a register of all charities)

○ a registered housing association other than a co-operative housing association

○ an unregistered housing association which is a co-operative housing association.

If before 15 January 1989 premises were occupied by a protected or statutory tenant (under the Rent Act 1977) and subsequently the landlord's interest is acquired by one of the public or quasi-public bodies listed above, the landlord condition required for the existence of a secure tenancy will be satisfied.

For tenancies created on or after 15 January 1989, the list of bodies which are now able to grant secure tenancies has been changed. The landlord must be one of the following:

○ a local authority
○ a new town corporation
○ an urban development corporation
○ the Development Board for Rural Wales

○ a housing action trust established under Part III of the Housing Act 1988

○ a housing co-operative.

Since the coming into force of the Housing Act 1988 new tenancies granted by the Housing Corporation, charitable housing trusts and (generally speaking) housing associations except fully mutual housing associations will be assured tenancies.

joint landlords

The premises occupied by the tenant may be jointly owned (for example, by two different local authorities or by a local authority and a housing association). In such situations, the landlord condition will only be satisfied if all the joint landlords fall within the statutory definition.

the occupier

It is in general irrelevant whether the occupier holds under a lease or a licence: the Housing Act 1985 gives the same protection to licensees as to tenants. Although the Act provides that a secure tenancy is a 'tenancy under which a dwelling-house is let as separate dwelling', it is also expressly stated that the secure tenancy provisions 'apply in relation to a licence to occupy a dwelling-house . . . as they apply in relation to a tenancy'. Therefore, the lease/licence distinction which is such a feature of the law in the private residential sector does not pose problems in the public sector.

There is, however, one exception to the proposition that a licensee may be a secure tenant. A secure tenancy cannot arise where a licence is given as a temporary expedient to someone who enters land as a trespasser.

(Throughout the pages which now follow, the terms secure tenant/tenancy are used to describe both tenants/tenancies and licensees/licences within the scope of the Housing Act 1985.)

individual occupier
The tenant must be an individual. If there is a joint tenancy, each tenant must be an individual. A limited company cannot be a secure tenant.

occupier's only or principal home
The occupier, in order to come within the secure tenancy scheme, must occupy the dwelling-house as his only or principal home. Where there is a joint tenancy, the tenant condition will be satisfied if one of the joint tenants lives in the property.

The requirement that the tenant must occupy the premises as his only or principal home is different from the Rent Act formula, according to which the tenant simply has to occupy the premises as his residence. Under the Rent Act 1977 a person might be regarded as residing in two places – in which case statutory protection would attach to both. This is not possible under the Housing Act 1985.

Nevertheless, the courts have, on occasion, interpreted the requirement that the tenant should occupy the premises as his only or principal home quite generously. In one case the following facts occurred: a tenant of a council house moved out of his council house in order to live with his girlfriend in 1985; in July 1986 he informed the council of this; in August 1986 the council gave the tenant notice to quit, by which time the tenant had split up with his girlfriend and he moved back into the council house in October.

Although during the previous twelve months the tenant had spent little time in the house, he had continued to pay the rent and rates, and visited the premises once a month. The court took the view that the tenant had been occupying his girlfriend's home on a temporary basis, and that the council house had remained his principal home throughout.

exclusions

By virtue of Schedule 1 to the Housing Act 1985 the following tenancies are not secure tenancies:

long leases

A long lease is a lease granted for 21 years or more, whether or not it can be terminated before the end of the term by the tenant serving a notice or by the landlord bringing forfeiture proceedings.

premises occupied in connection with employment

The situation covered by this exception is where the tenant is required by his contract of employment to occupy the dwelling-house for the better performance of his duties. The Act deals specifically with members of the police force and firemen. Policemen are not secure tenants if the accommodation is provided free of rent and rates. A tenancy granted to a fireman is excluded if the contract of employment requires him to live in close proximity to a particular fire station and the dwelling-house was let to him in consequence of that requirement.

land acquired for development

If the landlord acquires land for development but then lets it as temporary housing accommodation pending the development in question, there will be no secure tenancy.

accommodation for homeless persons

Part III of the Housing Act 1985 imposes various duties on local authorities with regard to homeless persons. If a person is being accommodated temporarily while the local authority considers whether there is a duty to house him under these 'housing the homeless' provisions in Part III of the Housing Act 1985, no secure tenancy arises. However, the accommodation may cease to be temporary for these purposes if the tenant occupies the premises for more than a year and a secure tenancy can then arise.

temporary accommodation for persons taking up employment

A person will not qualify as a secure tenant if he is given accommodation by a local authority in order to enable him to take up a new job. He may become a secure tenant if he remains in the property for more than a year.

short-term arrangements
Private sector bodies may let property to a landlord in the public sector, to be used as temporary housing accommodation. Tenancies granted in such circumstances by the public sector landlord are not secure tenancies.

temporary accommodation during works
A secure tenancy does not arise if a person is provided with temporary accommodation while the premises which he usually occupies, of which he is not a secure tenant, are being repaired.

agricultural holdings, licensed premises and almshouses
A dwelling that forms part of an agricultural holding, or one that consists of or includes licensed premises (a pub) will not provide a secure tenancy, nor will a person living in a charitable almshouse be a secure tenant.

student letting
A letting by one of the designated landlords to a student who attends a full-time course at a university, polytechnic or other college is not normally a secure tenancy, but the landlord must give notice to the student explaining the exemption.

If the student ceases to attend the course, or the course finishes and he stays on in the premises, the student occupier will become a secure tenant after six months from the date on which he ceased to attend the course, or the course finished. It is therefore important for the landlord to take possession proceedings as soon he becomes aware that either of these circumstances has arisen.

business premises
Tenancies of premises occupied for business purposes falling within Part II of the 1954 Act are not secure tenancies.

security of tenure

Secure tenants enjoy security of tenure analogous to that of private sector assured tenants under the Housing Act 1988 and regulated tenants under the Rent Act 1977. A secure tenant may continue to live in his home unless and until the landlord has obtained a court order to regain possession. The court will grant an order for possession only in certain prescribed circumstances.

periodic and fixed term tenancies

A secure tenancy may be granted as a contractual periodic tenancy (for example, week by week or month by month) or for a fixed term (such as for a year). A contractual periodic secure tenancy will continue until terminated by the tenant or by a court order.

When a secure tenant occupies premises under a tenancy for a fixed period, when the fixed term comes to an end, the tenant becomes entitled to a statutory periodic tenancy. Under the statutory periodic tenancy, the tenant continues to occupy the premises on the same terms as the original secure tenancy in so far as these terms are compatible with a periodic tenancy. The length of the period will depend on the period by reference to which the tenant has been paying rent: if monthly, the statutory periodic tenancy will be a monthly tenancy; if weekly, there will be a weekly tenancy and so on.

when the tenant wants to end a secure tenancy

There are a number of ways in which a tenant may bring a secure tenancy to an end:

notice to quit
A tenant may end a periodic secure tenancy (regardless of whether the tenancy is contractual or statutory) by serving a notice to quit on the landlord.

surrender
The landlord and tenant may agree that the tenancy should
come to an end.

right to buy
If the secure tenant exercises his 'right to buy' he becomes an
owner-occupier and the secure tenancy comes to an end. (The
'right to buy' is discussed in the next chapter of this book.)

when the landlord wants to end the secure tenancy

The landlord cannot bring a secure tenancy to an end without
an order of the court.

if it is a periodic tenancy
The only way in which the landlord may bring a periodic
secure tenancy to an end is by obtaining an order for possession from the court. Before the court will grant such an
order, a landlord must establish one of the 16 grounds for
possession listed in Schedule 2 to the Housing Act 1985. If the
landlord is granted an order for possession, the tenant must
vacate the premises.

if it is a fixed term tenancy
A fixed term tenancy will usually contain a clause giving the
landlord the right to forfeit the lease in certain circumstances
(in particular where the tenant is in breach of his obligations
under the terms of the tenancy).

If the landlord brings proceedings to terminate a fixed term
secure tenancy, the court may make one of two orders – for
termination, or for possession.

If the tenant is in breach of covenant – in which case the
landlord is entitled to forfeit the lease – the court may grant an
order terminating the contractual tenancy. Such an order does
not, however, entitle the landlord to recover possession.
Although the contractual tenancy is terminated by the order of

the court, a statutory periodic tenancy automatically arises and the tenant will be entitled to continue occupying the premises.

Alternatively, the court may grant an order for possession. In this case the tenant's right to occupy the premises ceases. Before the court will grant such an order, the landlord must establish one of the 16 grounds for possession listed in Schedule 2 to the Housing Act 1985.

procedure for landlord

A landlord who wishes to obtain an order for possession must first serve on the tenant notice in the prescribed form. There are two forms: one for use where the secure tenant has a periodic tenancy, the other for a fixed term tenancy.

Both forms state the name(s) of the secure tenant(s), the name of the landlord and address of the property, the ground on which possession is sought and the landlord's reasons for taking action to recover possession. There are extensive notes to explain the importance of the notice to the recipient. A notice in respect of a periodic tenancy also gives a date before which court proceedings cannot be brought.

the statutory grounds for obtaining possession

The Housing Act 1985 lays down the grounds on which a landlord may recover possession if the court considers it reasonable to do so. (The question of reasonableness does not arise for grounds 9, 10 and ll. For all the others, the court must consider reasonableness separately from the grounds.)

GROUND 1   *any rent lawfully due from a tenant has not been paid, or any obligation (such as to repair) has been broken or not performed*

Generally, the court will not regard it reasonable to make an order for possession if the tenant makes good his breach of covenant or pays off all arrears of rent before court proceedings start. Furthermore, local authorities often do not want to obtain possession but simply wish to recover the rent arrears. Orders for possession are therefore often suspended, pending the payment of the arrears at so-much per week in addition to the current rent. (Even if the full amount of the arrears is paid off, the tenant may still be liable for the costs of the local authority in bringing the action unless they agree not to proceed with it.)

Where the tenant is persistently late in paying rent, the landlord may genuinely want to recover possession, and in these circumstances the court may think it reasonable to make an order for possession even if the tenant pays off the arrears before the court hearing.

GROUND 2　*the tenant or any person living with him has been guilty of conduct which constitutes a nuisance or annoyance to neighbours or has been convicted of using the dwelling-house (or allowing it to be used) for immoral or illegal purposes*
If a secure tenant engages in drunken behaviour, abuse or violence, the landlord may seek possession on the basis of ground 2. If the tenant causes noise (such as playing loud music late at night or keeping a large number of dogs) this may be regarded as a nuisance or annoyance. However, ground 2 will not normally apply to isolated incidents. In any event, the court must be satisfied that it is reasonable to make the order.

GROUND 3　*the condition of the dwelling-house or any of the common parts has deteriorated due to the act or default of the tenant or any person living with him*
The tenant's failure to carry out repairs would qualify as a default within the meaning of this ground.

If the tenant has a lodger or sub-tenant who has caused the deterioration, the landlord has to show that the tenant has not taken reasonable steps to remove the lodger or sub-tenant.

GROUND 4   *the tenant or someone living with him has damaged furniture provided by the landlord*
Again, if the furniture has been damaged by a lodger or sub-tenant, the landlord has to show that the tenant has not taken reasonable steps to remove him.

GROUND 5   *the tenant induced the landlord to grant him the tenancy by making false statements*

GROUND 6   *the tenant has acquired his home by way of exchange and received a premium from or paid a premium to the exchanging tenant*

GROUND 7   *where the tenancy was originally granted as a result of the tenant's employment with the landlord and the landlord is one of the following bodies*

- a local authority
- the Commission for the New Towns
- a new town or urban development corporation
- the Development Board for Rural Wales
- the governors of an aided school

and the tenant's dwelling-house is part of premises used mainly for non-residential purposes, the landlord has to show that the tenant's conduct or that of a person living with him makes it wrong for him to continue to occupy them.

GROUND 8   *the tenant occupies (or the previous tenant occupied) the dwelling-house while works are (or were) executed on his previous home*
If the tenant (or the previous tenant) was a secure tenant of that home and promised to leave the present premises when the works on his previous home were finished he can be ordered to give up possession when those works are finished.

suitable alternative accommodation

A landlord may obtain a court order for possession on one of the following grounds, if suitable alternative accommodation will be available to the tenant when the order takes effect.

Alternative accommodation is suitable if it is let on a secure tenancy or a protected tenancy or an assured tenancy (but not an assured shorthold tenancy) and, in the opinion of the court, it is reasonably suitable to the needs of the tenant and his family. In determining this, the court must have regard to

- the nature of the accommodation which the landlord in practice allocates to someone with similar needs
- the distance of the accommodation from the workplace or school/college, and so on, of the tenant and any members of his family
- the distance of the accommodation from the home of any member of the tenant's family where being near is essential to the well-being of either the tenant or the member of his family
- the needs (as regards extent of accommodation) and the means of the tenant and his family
- the terms on which the accommodation is available and the terms of the secure tenancy
- where furniture is provided under the secure tenancy, whether it is to be provided for the tenant in the alternative accommodation and, if so, the nature of that furniture.

Where the landlord is not a local authority and produces a certificate from the local authority saying that they will provide suitable accommodation, this is conclusive that such accommodation will be available. Local authorities are normally reluctant to give such certificates.

The grounds for possession if suitable alternative accommodation is available are:

GROUND 9 *the dwelling-house is overcrowded within the meaning of Part X of the Housing Act 1985*

GROUND 10 *intention to demolish or reconstruct*
This ground arises where the landlord intends, within a reasonable time of obtaining possession, to demolish or reconstruct the building or carry out work on the building (or on land let with it) and cannot reasonably do so without obtaining possession of the secure tenant's home. There must be a settled and clearly defined intention to redevelop on the part of the landlord, not merely some vague plan for the future. The court might, for example, require the landlord to produce evidence of its intentions, such as builders' estimates.

GROUND 10A *dwelling in redevelopment scheme*
This ground arises where the dwelling-house is in an area which is subject to a redevelopment scheme within the terms of the Housing and Planning Act 1986.

GROUND 11 *the landlord is a charity and the tenant's continued occupation of the property conflicts with the objects of the charity.*

reasonableness and alternative accommodation

To obtain possession on one of the following grounds, the landlord must satisfy the court not only that it is reasonable to make an order for possession (as with grounds 1 to 8) but also (as with grounds 9, 10 and 11) that suitable alternative accommodation will be available to the tenant when the order becomes effective.

GROUND 12 *dwelling needed for employee*
The tenant was formerly an employee of the landlord (or one of the bodies specified in ground 7) and the dwelling-house is within the curtilage of a building consisting mainly of accom-

modation held by the landlord for non-housing purposes and is reasonably needed for one of its employees (or an employee of one of the specified bodies) in the future.

GROUND 13   *specially adapted dwelling*
The tenant occupies property specifically adapted for use by a physically disabled person, there is no longer a disabled person living there, and the landlord wants possession for occupation by such a person.

GROUND 14   *dwelling let for special circumstances*
The landlord is a housing association which lets only to people whose circumstances (other than financial) make it especially difficult for them to satisfy their need for housing, there is now no longer anyone with special circumstances living in the property or the present tenant has received a firm offer of suitable alternative accommodation from a local authority, and the premises are required to house someone with special circumstances.

GROUND 15   *dwelling in vicinity of special facilities*
The dwelling-house is one of a group which the landlord lets to people with special needs, and a social service or special facility is provided nearby to assist the tenants; the dwelling-house is now not occupied by a person with special needs, and the landlord requires the property for a person with special needs to live in.

So, a landlord who lets houses in a complex specially designed for the elderly may regain possession on this ground.

GROUND 16   ***the tenant has succeeded to the secure tenancy and the property is more extensive than is reasonably required by him***
The court must take into account the tenant's age, the length of occupation of the dwelling, and any financial or other support

given by the tenant to the previous tenant. To recover possession on this ground, the landlord must bring proceedings between six and twelve months from the death of the previous tenant. A spouse of the deceased tenant cannot be dispossessed on this ground.

powers of the court

Where the landlord is seeking possession on one of the grounds which requires the court to be satisfied that it is reasonable to make an order for possession (that is, grounds 1 to 8 and 12 to 16) the court has a general power to adjourn proceedings. Furthermore, the court may stay or suspend an order for possession, and in such a case the court may impose conditions (such as in relation to the carrying out of repairs).

successors

If a secure tenant dies (before or after the end of the original occupation agreement), generally the tenancy is automatically transferred to the person entitled to succeed to the secure tenancy under the Housing Act 1985. Although there are some similarities between the succession provisions in the Housing Act 1985 and those contained in the Rent Act 1977, there are also some important differences. Under the Housing Act 1985 there is only one automatic successor; nothing in the Act, however, prevents a landlord from agreeing to a second succession.

who may succeed?

A person may succeed a secure tenant if at the time of the secure tenant's death he (or she) occupied the dwelling-house as his (or her) only or principal home and is either

○ the secure tenant's husband or wife; or
○ another member of the secure tenant's family and has lived

with the secure tenant throughout the 12 months up to the secure tenant's death.

The other members of the secure tenant's family (which includes illegitimate and adopted children and relations by marriage) are:

- a person who lives with the secure tenant as husband or wife (sometimes referred to as a 'common-law' husband or wife; this does not extend to partners of the same sex)
- parents, grandparents, grandchildren, children
- brothers and sisters
- uncles, aunts, nephews and nieces.

In order to satisfy the twelve months' residence require-ment, the successor must not only have lived with the former secure tenant but must have occupied the premises in ques-tion. The importance of this was revealed in the case of *South Northampton DC v Power*. In this case, Mr Power started living with Mrs Tulloch in 1982 in the house which was Mrs Tulloch's former matrimonial home. When Mrs Tulloch became a secure tenant of a council property in 1985, both Mrs Tulloch and Mr Power moved into these premises. Mrs Tulloch died nine months later, and the question arose as to whether Mr Power was entitled to succeed to the secure tenancy. The court held that although he had lived with Mrs Tulloch for a number of years, Mr Power was not entitled to succeed since he had not resided in the local authority premises during the previous twelve months.

priority of succession

A secure tenant's spouse takes precedence over other mem-bers of the family. If two or more members of the family are entitled to succeed to the secure tenancy (such as two children who were living with the secure tenant in the year prior to his death) and they cannot agree between themselves who is to become the new secure tenant by succession, the landlord can decide who is to be the successor.

no successors

In the following circumstances there will be no automatic transfer on the death of the secure tenant:

○ where there has already been an automatic transfer to a secure tenant's spouse or a member of his family; or
○ where the deceased secure tenant acquired the tenancy under the will or intestacy of the previous tenant; or
○ on the death of a surviving joint tenant (where there is joint tenancy and one tenant dies, the tenancy automatically passes to the survivor under the general law); or
○ where there was originally a fixed term or periodic tenancy which has been assigned (that is, sold or exchanged); although the assignee will be statutorily entitled to a periodic tenancy when the original term ends, there is no automatic transfer on his death.

There are, however, exceptions to the rule that there can be no succession on the death of an assignee:

– assignees who take over the secure tenancy under a property transfer order on or after a divorce, nullity or judicial separation, do not count as assignees for the purpose of the succession provisions (unless the other party to the marriage had acquired the tenancy by assignment)
– on the death of an assignee by way of exchange there may be a succession to the secure tenancy as long as the tenant by way of exchange was not a successor to the premises which he exchanged.

Where on the death of the secure tenant there is no automatic entitlement to succeed to the secure tenancy, the tenancy will pass to the person entitled under the deceased's will or under intestacy rules. The tenancy, however, ceases to be secure. In such a situation, the landlord may bring proceedings with a view to terminating the tenancy and recovering possession under the common law. In relation to a periodic tenancy, the landlord may terminate a tenancy by serving a notice to quit. If the tenancy is for a fixed term, the landlord will be able to recover possession at the end of the fixed term; during the fixed term itself the landlord may institute forfeiture proceedings if the tenant is in breach of covenant.

spouses

The position of spouses has been mentioned in the context of succession to a secure tenancy and the next pages draw together the various provisions which specifically apply to married couples.

a spouse's right of occupation
If a married couple are joint tenants they both have a right to occupy the home by virtue of their legal rights as tenants. The law also provides that where one spouse is entitled to occupy the matrimonial home by virtue of being a secure tenant, the other spouse, although not a tenant, also has a right of occupation in the dwelling. The non-tenant spouse may apply to the court to enforce his or her rights of occupation.

deserted spouse
One of the conditions necessary for a secure tenancy is that the tenant must occupy the premises as his only or principal home. If the husband, who is a secure tenant, abandons the matrimonial home, does the tenancy cease to be secure? In relation to the matrimonial home, occupation by the deserted (non-tenant) spouse is regarded as equivalent to occupation by the tenant, and the landlord cannot refuse to accept rent from whichever tenant is in occupation. So, a deserted spouse can remain in occupation – even though not a tenant – as long as he or she keeps paying the rent.

This protection continues only while the marriage is subsisting. If the non-tenant spouse wishes to remain in occupation after the marriage has come to an end, he or she should apply for a transfer of the tenancy.

marriage breakdown

On the break-up of a marriage, the courts have a broad discretion to adjust the property rights of the husband and wife. On a decree of divorce, nullity or judicial separation or at any time thereafter the court has the power to order a transfer of a secure tenancy from one spouse to the other.

In practical terms, it is important that the court should order a transfer of the tenancy in the context of the divorce proceedings, since problems may arise if the marriage comes to an end before the tenancy is transferred. In the situation where the husband is the secure tenant, and the ex-wife continues to occupy the council premises after the divorce, the tenancy ceases to be secure (because the tenant no longer occupies the premises as his only or principal home), and therefore the court cannot transfer the tenancy to the wife. If, however, after the divorce the secure tenant remains in occupation, the tenancy continues to be secure and the court retains its power to transfer it to the other spouse. After the transfer, the spouse to whom the secure tenancy has been transferred becomes a secure tenant.

death of the spouse

There are three different factual situations which must be distinguished.

First, if the spouses were joint tenants, the survivor automatically becomes the sole secure tenant on the death of the other spouse. There can be no succession, however, on the survivor's death – even if the survivor remarries.

Secondly, if the deceased was a secure tenant, the surviving spouse is entitled to succeed to the secure tenancy as long as the following conditions are satisfied:

- he or she was living with the secure tenant at the time of the tenant's death
- the deceased tenant was the original tenant, rather than a successor.

Thirdly, if the deceased tenant was a successor to the secure tenancy, the surviving spouse is not entitled to succeed to the secure tenancy. In this case, although the tenancy will pass to someone (often the spouse) by virtue of the law of succession (either under the former secure tenant's will (if any) or under intestacy rules), the tenancy ceases to be secure. Accordingly, the landlord may take action to terminate the tenancy and recover possession under the common law.

unmarried couples

The provisions outlined above do not apply to unmarried couples. For example, an unmarried couple occupies a council house; the man is a periodic secure tenant; the man leaves the premises and stops paying the rent. First, the woman does not have a right of occupation since she is not married to the tenant. Secondly, since it is a condition of a secure tenancy that the tenant should occupy the dwelling-house as his only or principal home, the tenancy ceases to be secure when the man leaves. Thirdly, the woman cannot apply to the court for an order transferring the tenancy to her. So, the woman in occupation has no security of tenure, and the local authority can terminate the tenancy and may bring proceedings in order to recover possession of the house.

These problems would not arise if at the outset the local authority granted the secure tenancy to the unmarried couple jointly.

– on death

As regards succession to a statutory tenancy, a cohabiting partner (but not a partner of the same sex) may succeed if:

- he or she lived with the deceased tenant in the premises in question for the twelve months prior to the former tenant's death; and
- the deceased tenant was not a successor to the secure tenancy.

rights of a secure tenant (apart from the right to buy)

None of the tenant's rights can be excluded by the tenancy agreement. (The right to buy is discussed in the next chapter.)

the right to exchange

Secure tenants may exchange their homes with other secure tenants. There is no need for the two secure tenants to have the same landlord. Obtaining the landlord's written consent is a pre-condition to exchange; where the secure tenants have different landlords, the consent of both landlords is required.

The landlord may refuse consent only on one of the grounds listed below, and must give his tenant notice of such refusal within 42 days of the tenant applying for consent. If the consent is withheld for some other reason, it will be treated as having been given. When giving consent, the landlord may impose a condition on the tenant that any arrears of rent must be paid or that any breaches of the terms of the tenancy must be remedied. No other conditions may be imposed.

Consent to exchange can be refused if:

o a possession order has been made against the landlord's existing tenant or the person with whom he hopes to exchange ('the tenant by way of exchange')
o possession proceedings have been started against the tenant or the tenant by way of exchange on one of the grounds relating to a tenant's default under his lease (that is, grounds 1 to 6 which include failure to pay rent, damage to furniture and so on)
o the tenant by way of exchange would have substantially more accommodation than he reasonably requires
o the accommodation is not suitable for the needs of the tenant by way of exchange and his family

○ the premises are within the curtilage of a building held by a landlord for non-residential purposes and are let to the tenant in consequence of his employment with either the landlord or another designated public body (if the employee is required to occupy the property for the better fulfilment of his job he is not a secure tenant)

○ the dwelling-house is let by a charity and occupation by the proposed tenant by way of exchange would result in a breach of the charity's objects

○ the property is specially adapted for a physically disabled person and the result of the exchange would be that such a person would no longer occupy the property

○ the landlord is a housing association or housing trust which lets the property only to people whose circumstances (other than financial circumstances) make them difficult to house and the exchange would mean that such a person would no longer live in the property

○ the property is one of a group set up for people with special needs near to specially provided facilities or social services and the exchange would mean that the property would no longer be occupied by a person with such special needs.

A secure tenant should not take any lump sum payment on exchange. If he does, the landlord may be able to recover possession and would not have to provide alternative accommodation.

the right to take in lodgers

A secure tenant may take in lodgers without obtaining the landlord's prior consent. However, if the house becomes overcrowded within the meaning of the Housing Act 1985 as a consequence, the landlord may be entitled to obtain possession of it.

the right to sub-let

Every secure tenant has the right to sub-let part of his home. He must first obtain his landlord's consent, which cannot be unreasonably withheld. If consent is withheld unreasonably, the consent is treated as having been given. The onus is on the landlord to show that the withholding was not unreasonable.

If the landlord refuses consent, the tenant can demand a written statement of the reasons for such refusal. If the landlord gives consent conditionally (for example, subject to the tenant doing repairs) the consent takes effect as if the condition did not exist. If the landlord neither gives nor refuses consent but merely remains silent, he will be deemed to have withheld consent unreasonably.

Where a secure tenant feels that his landlord has unreasonably refused consent or remained silent, the most sensible thing for him to do is to apply to the county court for a declaration of consent having been unreasonably withheld. He may then sub-let without risk of being in breach of the terms of his lease.

If a secure tenant sub-lets the whole of his home, he ceases to be a secure tenant (as he no longer occupies the premises as his home), and therefore he loses the protection of the Housing Act 1985. The sub-tenant in such circumstances does not qualify as a secure tenant either.

the right to make improvements

The right to make improvements is subject to the tenant first obtaining the landlord's consent in writing. Consent must not be unreasonably withheld, and if it is it will be deemed to have been given. The onus is on the landlord to show that the withholding of consent is reasonable. If consent is withheld, the landlord must give the tenant a written statement explaining why.

If the landlord gives consent to the improvements, conditions may be imposed provided that they are reasonable. A secure tenant is in breach of his obligations under the lease (and therefore runs the risk of the landlord bringing possession proceedings) if he fails to comply with a reasonable condition. If, however, the landlord gives consent subject to an unreasonable condition, the law regards the consent as having been unreasonably withheld.

The Housing Act 1985 enables the landlord to repay to the secure tenant at, or after, the end of the tenancy, some or all of the costs of the improvement, though there is no duty to do so. The landlord may do so where:

○ the improvement was made after 3 October 1980
○ the landlord gave consent to the improvement
○ the improvement materially added to the price which the property would be expected to reach if sold or rented on the open market.

A landlord is not allowed to increase the rent to take account of the tenant's improvements, except to the extent that the tenant did not bear the cost of the improvements himself. But, where the tenant pays rent inclusive of rates, he will have to bear the expense of any increase in rates resulting from the improvements. A secure tenant's successor is also protected from any increase in rent because of improvements made by his predecessor. Only when the successor's tenancy ends can the landlord increase the rent payable in respect of the improved property.

the right to be consulted

Secure tenants have the right to be consulted by their landlord on most aspects of housing management. If a landlord proposes to make substantial alterations to the layout of an estate, for instance, the tenants must be consulted, and their views considered, before a decision is taken. Landlords must, on request, provide their secure tenants with details of their consultation procedure.

the right to carry out repairs

The repairing obligations of landlords, and tenants' rights and remedies, are discussed in the last chapter of the book.

the right to information

Tenants' rights to information are also discussed in the last chapter.

the right to assign

In general, the assignment (that is, transfer) of secure tenancies is not permitted and a tenancy will cease to be a secure tenancy if it is assigned. There are, however, three exceptions to this:

○ a secure tenancy may sometimes be assigned by way of exchange
○ a secure tenancy may be assigned during divorce proceedings
○ a secure tenancy may be assigned to a person who would be entitled to succeed to the secure tenancy on the death of the secure tenant.

exclusion

The statutory rights just mentioned – the rights to exchange, to take in lodgers, to sublet, to improve, to repair, the rights to be consulted and the right to information – do not apply to certain secure tenancies, namely where the landlord is a co-operative housing association not registered under the Housing Associations Act 1985 and the tenancy was created before 15 January 1989.

other terms of a secure tenancy

While the various statutory rights given to secure tenants by the Housing Act 1985 cannot be excluded by the provisions of the lease, in principle all the other terms of a secure tenancy (including rent) can be freely negotiated by the landlord and tenant. In practice, of course, council tenants enter tenancies on the terms used by the public authority in its standard form tenancy agreement.

rent

Whereas under the Rent Act 1977 rents are subject to statutory control, there is, in general, no such control in the public sector. (In relation to housing association tenancies as defined by Part VI of the Rent Act 1977, the system of rent control which governs regulated tenancies applies.)

As regards council tenancies, the local authority enjoys a broad discretion to determine the level of rents according to social policy. It is not obliged to charge economic rents, nor is it obliged to charge non-economic rents. Although a local authority may subsidise rents, it is not under a duty to do so. The council must balance the interests of the tenants and the body of rate-payers as a whole.

In a number of cases, rate-payers and tenants have challenged rents fixed by the local authority by way of judicial review on the ground that they are unreasonable. In only one case has such a challenge been successful. The courts will not interfere with the exercise by the local authority of its discretion in this respect, unless the local authority has made a decision which no reasonable authority could have taken.

variation of terms

Once a tenancy has been entered into, the terms agreed

continue to bind the parties until the end of the tenancy unless they are altered. It is a basic principle of the law of contract that the terms of a contract cannot be altered without the consent of both parties. On this principle, therefore, the terms of a tenancy can be changed either according to the agreed terms of the lease itself or by agreement.

In relation to public sector housing, there are special statutory provisions which set out the ways in which the terms of secure tenancies can be varied. Sections 102 to 103 of the Housing Act 1985 provide for the terms of a secure tenancy to be altered in one of the following ways:

○ by agreement between the landlord and the tenant
○ in relation to payments for rent, rates and services, in accordance with the terms of the tenancy
○ in the case of a periodic tenancy, by notice of variation.

With regard to this last, the landlord serves notice of the variation on the tenant, explaining the substance of the variation and asking the tenant for his comments. After considering the tenant's comments, the landlord serves a further notice on the tenant which states the date on which the variation is to take effect: this must be either when a rental period expires or after four weeks, whichever is longer. The tenant's sole remedy, if he objects to the variation, is to give notice to quit.

The landlord does not need to observe the procedure of a preliminary notice when issuing a variation notice regarding payments in respect of rent, rates or services.

PUBLIC SECTOR TENANTS' RIGHT TO BUY

In the context of public sector housing, one of the most radical changes in recent years has been the introduction of the right to buy for most categories of secure tenant. The right of public sector tenants to buy their homes was created by the Housing Act 1980; it is now contained in the Housing Act 1985. This lays down in considerable detail the conditions which have to be satisfied in order for the right to buy to arise, what the secure tenant can buy, the terms on which the sale has to be made, the method for determining the price to be paid, and the procedure which has to be adopted if the right to buy is to be exercised.

The law also gives a right to a mortgage to public sector tenants who wish to exercise the right to buy. There are further provisions relating to, amongst other things, shared ownership leases (whereby a secure tenant may purchase his home in 'slices').

who has the right to buy and when

In order to have the right to buy the secure tenant must have been a tenant of a public sector landlord for at least two years. The two year period does not need to have been spent in the same dwelling-house nor as a tenant of the same landlord. The important point is that the time should have been spent as a public sector tenant.

joint tenants and members of the family

When two or more secure joint tenants are entitled to buy their home, the right belongs to them all jointly. At least one of them must occupy the dwelling as his only or principal home. Only one of the joint tenants needs to have satisfied the time condition.

When the secure tenant gives notice of his intention to buy the premises which he occupies, up to three members of his family (who need not be joint tenants) may be allowed to buy with him. But family members who have not lived with the tenant for the previous twelve months may join in the purchase only if the landlord gives his consent.

exclusions

The Housing Act 1985 excludes the following secure tenancies from the right to buy provisions:

○ lettings by a housing trust or housing association where the landlord is a charity
○ lettings by co-operative housing associations or other housing associations which have at no point received public funds
○ lettings by landlords with an insufficient interest to grant a long lease to the tenant: as regards houses, in order to have a sufficient interest, the landlord must be the freehold owner or hold a lease of more than twenty-one years; in relation to flats, the landlord must own either the freehold of the building or a lease of the flat for a period of at least fifty years
○ lettings of properties which are held mainly for non-housing purposes and which were let to the tenant or his predecessor in connection with his employment
○ certain lettings of properties specially adapted for physically disabled persons
○ lettings of sheltered accommodation for mentally disordered persons

- ○ certain lettings of property adapted for use by the elderly
- ○ certain lettings by the Crown.

secure tenants who cannot exercise the right to buy
The Housing Act also provides that the right to buy cannot be exercised by any of the following:

- ○ a tenant against whom an order for possession has been made (whether or not the tenant has given up possession)
- ○ a tenant who is an undischarged bankrupt or who has a bankruptcy petition pending against him or has a receiving order in force against him or has made a composition or arrangement with his creditors the terms of which remain to be fulfilled.

what a secure tenant can buy

The law treats houses and flats differently.

houses

If the secure tenant lives in a house and the landlord owns the freehold, the tenant is entitled to acquire the freehold interest. If the landlord only owns a leasehold interest, the tenant will be granted a long lease at a nominal rent. Normally, the lease will be for a period of at least 125 years; it will be for less where the landlord's own interest is for a shorter period.

A tenant who is granted a long lease of a house might at a later date be able to 'enfranchise' his interest and acquire the freehold under the Leasehold Reform Act 1967, even where the freehold is owned by someone in the private sector.

flats

If the secure tenant lives in a flat, he will be granted a long lease at a nominal rent; again the lease will normally be for at least 125 years, although sometimes it may be for less.

terms

Where a tenant on exercising the right to buy is granted a long lease by the landlord, the following provisions will be contained (or implied) in it:

○ rights to the enjoyment of common parts previously enjoyed by the secure tenant

○ an obligation on the landlord to keep the structure and exterior of the dwelling-house in repair and make good any defect affecting that structure, unless details of such defects have been given to the tenant

○ an indemnity by the tenant in respect of restrictive covenants affecting the landlord

○ a covenant by the tenant to keep the interior in repair

○ rights of support, passage of water, gas, electricity etc.

○ necessary rights of way

○ other rights enjoyed by the tenant when he gave notice of intent to buy, insofar as the landlord can grant them.

Some of these rights (such as the last three) will also be included in a conveyance of the freehold of a house to a secure tenant who is exercising his right to buy, where appropriate.

calculating the price

The Housing Act 1985 lays down the method for calculating the price that the secure tenant must pay when buying his home. The formula is: the value of the dwelling-house at the relevant time, less the discount to which the tenant is entitled.

The 'relevant time' is the date at which the secure tenant serves a notice on the landlord of his intention to buy.

The value of the dwelling-house means the price that it would realise if sold on the open market by a willing seller. In the case of a sale of the freehold interest, the following assumptions are made:

○ the vendor is selling the freehold with vacant possession
○ neither the tenant nor a member of his family living there with him wants to buy
○ the property is to be conveyed subject only to rights and burdens which may be imposed under the Housing Act 1985; these include necessary rights of way, rights of support and light and passage of water, gas and electricity, sewage and so on.

On the grant of a long lease (that is, where the home is a flat or where the landlord owns only a leasehold interest, if it is a house) the assumptions are that:

○ the ground rent will not exceed £10 per annum
○ where the landlord has an interest of more than 125 years plus five days, he is granting a lease of 125 years with vacant possession
○ where the landlord has an interest of less than 125 years and five days, he is granting a lease equal to the remainder of his own term less five days, with vacant possession
○ neither the tenant nor a member of his family living there with him wants to take the lease
○ the grant is on the terms specified in the Housing Act 1985.

The effect of these assumptions is to lower the price which the property would otherwise realise if sold to the secure tenant.

In making the valuation, any improvements made by the secure tenant or a member of his family or predecessors (if they had been secure tenants) are ignored.

In the first instance, it is the responsibility of the landlord to determine the value of the dwelling-house at the relevant time.

A landlord may ask the district valuer to help in this respect. If the district valuer is not initially consulted, or if the tenant disagrees with the value attributed to the dwelling by the landlord or the district valuer, the tenant has the right to require a revaluation to be carried out by another officer from the district valuer's office. A tenant must serve written notice on his landlord within three months of receiving the landlord's valuation, requiring the district valuer's involvement.

the discount

The discount entitlement is calculated according to the length of time the secure tenant has been a public sector tenant. Periods as a tenant of many public sector landlords – not just the one from which the tenant wishes to buy – may be taken into account. Time spent by members of the secure tenant's family may also be taken into account, although it is not possible to add together different people's discount entitlements. If there is a secure joint tenancy, the discount is based on whichever of the joint tenants is entitled to the largest amount.

The discount entitlement for houses is as follows:

○ if the tenant has been a public sector tenant for two years, 32% of the value of the dwelling-house at the relevant time
○ for every completed year thereafter, an extra 1% is added to the amount of the discount, subject to a maximum of 60%.

The discount entitlement for flats is as follows:

○ if the tenant has been a public sector tenant for two years, 44% of the value of the dwelling-house at the relevant time
○ for every completed year thereafter, an extra 2% is added to the amount of the discount, subject to a maximum of 70%.

The maximum discount allowable is, in any circumstances, £50,000.

example

Jane Taylor has lived in her council house for ten years and at the date she makes her application it is valued at £60,000.

She will pay £60,000 less £24,000 (discount of 40%) amounting to £36,000.

Jim Thomson has lived in a flat for ten years – valued at £45,000. He will pay £45,000 less £27,000 (discount of 60%) amounting to £18,000.

used-up discount
A secure tenant's discount will be reduced if he has on a previous occasion exercised the right to buy and received a discount on that occasion (or if he has received a discount when acquiring a shared ownership lease). Similarly, the discount will be reduced where the tenant's spouse or other joint purchaser has received a discount on a prior occasion.

paying back the discount
A secure tenant who buys his home at a discount and then sells it to someone else within three years is liable to repay some or all of the discount he has received. The discount will be repayable in most cases involving sale, assignment and subletting for a period of more than twenty-one years. There is, however, a category of exempted disposals where the discount is not repayable. Exempted disposals include:

- a disposal to a spouse or resident members of the family who have lived with the tenant for a year or more
- a disposal to someone who could have bought (or who does buy) compulsorily
- a disposal of part of the property not including the residential part
- a disposal by will, or on a divorce following a court order made under section 24 of the Matrimonial Causes Act 1973. An order under section 24 is normally made where one of the parties continues to occupy the former matrimonial home after the divorce. If sale of the house follows an order not made under section 24, the discount (or part of it) will be repayable.

The amount to be repaid depends on when the sale, assignment or sub-letting takes place:

sale made	*discount repayable*
in the first year	the whole discount
in the second year	two-thirds
in the third year	one-third

So, if Jane Taylor in the first example above tries to make a quick profit by selling her house in the second year after she bought it, she will be liable to repay two-thirds of £24,000 – that is £16,000.

In some cases, a secure tenant does not have an unrestricted right to sell after three years. In certain rural areas, in particular areas of outstanding natural beauty and National Parks, there are restrictions on the persons to whom a secure tenant who has bought his home can sell it – for example, only to someone who lives or works in the area. In these areas, the possibility of such a restriction is taken into account in valuing the house or flat at the relevant time.

choosing the time for buying and selling

It is not necessarily in the best interests of the tenant to serve a notice of intention to exercise his right to buy at the earliest opportunity, because for every extra year he waits he will get an extra 1% discount. For example, on a property valued at £50,000 this means an extra £500 discount for every year.

A tenant should therefore be aware of the precise date on which his qualifying occupation began, because it could be a matter of only days whether or not he gets an extra 1% discount.

Against this has to be weighed that the valuation is based on the date on which the tenant serves notice of his intention to buy, and property prices normally rise by more than 1% per year. So, while it may be worth the tenant waiting for a few days, it may not be worth delaying for, say, a year.

As for selling, the tenant should, within the first three years, consider carefully whether he should wait until the expiration of a further year before selling.

the procedure

The tenant serves *Notice Claiming the Right to Buy* on his landlord (form RTB 1). The landlord has to supply form RTB 1 within seven days of receiving a request for it.

Form RTB 1 comprises seven sections asking for details of the property, the tenant, members of the tenant's family who wish to share the right to buy, the periods of occupation which will count towards establishing the right to buy and calculating the discount, any previous purchase at a discount from a public sector landlord, particulars of any improvements made to the property. Form RTB 1 also explains what will happen next.

Within four weeks of receiving form RTB 1, the landlord must serve *Notice in Reply to Tenant's Right to Buy Claim* (form RTB 2). The period is eight weeks if the two-year qualifying period includes a period as the tenant of a different landlord.

On form RTB 2, the landlord inserts the names of those secure tenants whose claim to buy he admits, and of those whose claim he denies, with the reasons for denying the claim.

If a landlord denies the tenant's claim, the tenant can seek legal advice from a citizens advice bureau or legal advice centre. He can go to the county court to try to establish his rights. A free booklet *Your right to buy your home* published by the Department of the Environment contains guidance and explains how to get help and advice if needed.

notice of the terms of the sale

If the landlord admits the tenant's claim or the tenant success-fully establishes his right, the landlord must send a notice stating the proposed terms of sale. The notice must be served by the landlord within eight weeks of the service of form RTB 2 (in the case of a freehold purchase) or twelve weeks (in cases where a lease is being granted).

The notice must state the price, and how it was calculated; tenant's improvements which have been disregarded; the discount entitlement, and how this was calculated; provisions to be included in the conveyance or lease. If the landlord is to grant a lease and there will be a service charge, an estimate of that charge has to be given.

The notice must also contain an explanation of the tenant's right to have the value of the property determined or redetermined by the district valuer, details of the tenant's right to a mortgage, details of the notice to complete procedure, details of the tenant's right to defer completion and details of the shared ownership lease scheme.

dealing with delays

The landlord has to deal with the completion of the conveyance or the grant of the lease as quickly as circumstances allow. Naturally, the tenant's mortgage arrangements must be finalised and the terms of the conveyance or lease agreed but, after that, if the landlord unreasonably delays, the tenant can ask the Secretary of State to exercise his default powers to push through the conveyance or the grant of the lease.

Where a secure tenant claims a mortgage and this is not enough to meet all the costs of his purchase, he may be able to defer completion of the sale. The tenant must serve on the landlord notice of his wish to defer completion until he can find the extra money to meet all his costs, within three months of receiving his mortgage offer; a longer period may be allowed where reasonable. He must also pay a deposit of £100. The deposit is returnable if the sale does not go ahead; if the sale does go ahead, it will count towards the purchase price. The maximum time for which completion can be delayed is two years from the date of service of form RTB 1. A tenant who has the right to defer completion may also be entitled to claim a shared ownership lease.

the first notice to complete

If the tenant delays completing after certain time limits have elapsed, the landlord can serve the tenant with a notice (the 'first notice to complete') requiring him to state whether the delay is due to outstanding matters in respect of a mortgage or other relevant matters. The tenant is given a reasonable time (at least 56 days) in which to reply. The landlord's notice also states what will happen to the tenant's claim if he fails to comply with a second notice to complete, should the landlord subsequently serve one.

The notice requiring an explanation for delay cannot be served

○ where the value of the dwelling remains to be finally determined (an example would be where the tenant has asked for a determination by the district valuer)
○ if the tenant has not claimed a mortgage, unless nine months have passed since he first could have claimed the mortgage
○ during any period in which the tenant has exercised his right to defer completion
○ while the tenant is claiming a shared ownership lease.

the second notice to complete

If the landlord gets no reasonable explanation for the delay, he may serve the 'second notice to complete' on the tenant asking him to complete within the period stated in the notice. This must be a reasonable period, with a minimum of 56 days, and the period can be extended by the landlord. If the tenant does not complete within the stated time, he is treated as having withdrawn his claim to buy his home.

A second notice to complete cannot be served on a tenant who claims a shared ownership lease.

withdrawing a claim

A secure tenant may withdraw his claim at any time by giving written notice (forms are available from law stationers) to his landlord. Theoretically, he may withdraw his claim one day and put in a new claim the next.

cost to the tenant

The tenant usually has to meet the following expenses in addition to the purchase price:

○ his own costs of employing a surveyor and a solicitor
○ the legal costs incurred in obtaining a mortgage
○ stamp duty (at present 1% of the price paid where the purchase price is more than £30,000)
○ Land Registry fees.

Land Registry fees are payable because a tenant who buys his home under the Housing Act 1985 has to register the title with the appropriate district land registry. The fee depends on the value of the property.

procedural problems

In view of the length of time which it may take between the tenant serving his intention to exercise his right to buy and the completion of the sale, there are potential problems if the tenant's status changes during the course of the procedure.

the tenant ceasing to be a secure tenant

It has been held by the courts that the right to buy only continues while the tenant is a secure tenant. Accordingly, if a secure tenant serves the landlord with notice of his intention to exercise the right to buy but subsequently the tenancy ceases to be secure (for example, as a result of the tenant ceasing to occupy the premises as his only or principal home) the tenant is no longer entitled to exercise the right to buy.

the landlord becoming entitled to possession during the course of the procedure

A similar problem arises when, at some point after the tenant has served on the landlord notice of his intention to exercise the right to buy, the landlord becomes entitled to an order for possession on one of the grounds set out in Schedule 2 to the Housing Act 1985.

The right to buy cannot be exercised by a person against whom an order for possession has been obtained. The question is, however: at what point is the right to buy deemed to be exercised? If it is exercised once and for all when the tenant serves the necessary notice on the landlord setting the whole procedure in motion, the landlord subsequently becoming entitled to possession (for example, on the basis of the tenant's failure to pay rent) would be irrelevant.

The courts have decided that the tenant serving the necessary notice and the landlord accepting the tenant's right to buy cannot be equated with the tenant having exercised the right. Only when the tenant takes some step towards implementing completion of the purchase (such as requisitioning the mortgage money, perhaps) can it be said that the tenant has irrevocably exercised his right to buy. If the landlord becomes entitled to possession between notice and completion, the tenant is precluded from exercising (or continuing to exercise) his right to buy.

It is therefore important that while seeking to purchase his home, the secure tenant continues to pay rent and to comply with his obligations under the tenancy.

the right to a mortgage

A secure tenant who has the right to buy his home also has the right to obtain a mortgage from or through the local authority to finance the purchase. Where the tenant's landlord is a housing association, the mortgage is provided by the Housing Corporation.

Where two or more tenants have the right to buy, a mortgage can be obtained jointly by all of them. By pooling their income they may be able to get a larger mortgage than a sole secure tenant.

The landlord and tenant may agree on the terms of the mortgage. If there is no such agreement the following terms apply regarding the amount and length of the mortgage.

how much

The amount that the tenant can borrow depends on two issues. First, the mortgage cannot exceed the purchase price, plus such of the landlord's costs as are chargeable to the tenant and any costs incurred by the tenant and defrayed by the landlord.

Second, the amount will be reduced if the tenant's relevant income (or, in the case of a joint application, the aggregate income) is insufficient. The relevant income is established by calculating the applicant's annual income from all sources, minus (where applicable) an amount equal to the annual payments made under any maintenance agreement, court order and credit agreement, which are likely to continue for the next 18 months or more. This gives the tenant's 'available annual income' which is then multiplied by a number (the multiplier). This multiplier depends on the applicant's age at the time he serves the notice indicating his desire to exercise the right to buy. The multiplier is 2.5 for someone under 60; it is 2 for someone aged between 60 and 64 and for people over 65 it is 1 (ie just the available annual income).

Where two or more joint tenants have the right to buy, their separate available annual incomes, calculated in the way just described, may be added together.

how long

The term over which the secure tenant should repay the mortgage is 25 years, but the tenant may opt for a shorter period and the landlord may extend it by agreement. If the tenant buys a leasehold interest of less than 25 years, the mortgage term will be the same as the period of the lease.

interest rate

The Housing Act 1985 specifies the rate of interest chargeable where the secure tenant buys from a local authority. The rate is whichever is the higher of the standard national rate as declared by the Secretary of State, or the applicable local average rate (broadly speaking one-quarter per cent above the rate paid by the local authority to borrow the money).

A secure tenant who buys from a public sector landlord other than a local authority should write to the landlord or the Housing Corporation for an estimate of the initial interest rate.

The interest rate may vary during the mortgage term, regardless of who the landlord is.

applying for a mortgage

A secure tenant buying from a housing association claims a mortgage by serving notice in the prescribed form on the Housing Corporation (149 Tottenham Court Road, London W1P 0BN).

All other secure tenants serve notice claiming a mortgage on their landlords. The prescribed form *Notice Claiming the Right to a Mortgage* (form No. 4) must be sent to a tenant by his landlord along with the notice of terms of sale. The form asks for details of a secure tenant's income, and of commitments to be deducted in calculating the tenant's available annual income.

The form must be served on the landlord (or the Housing Corporation, if appropriate) within three months of receiving the landlord's notice of terms of sale, or the determination of the value of the house by the district valuer where the value is disputed. The period may be extended if there are reasonable grounds for doing so.

A landlord or the Housing Corporation must reply to a tenant's claim on Form 4 'as soon as practicable'. The reply must state:

○ the amount which in the opinion of the landlord or the Housing Corporation the tenant is entitled to have advanced
○ the method used to calculate the amount
○ the provisions which the landlord or the Housing Corporation feel should be included in the mortgage deed.

A statement must accompany the landlord's (or the Housing Corporation's) reply, informing the tenant of his right to defer completion or to take a shared ownership lease if his income does not qualify him for a full 100% mortgage.

other sources of finance

There is nothing to stop a secure tenant from seeking a mortgage from sources other than his landlord (or the Housing Corporation), such as building societies, banks, insurance companies and so on, to finance his right to buy. But the tenant does not have a statutory right to a mortgage from these sources. In times of mortgage shortage, the availability of a mortgage from the landlord may be particularly important to an older tenant, say above 50 years, if other lenders would not be prepared to lend to a person of that age.

shared ownership leases

In certain circumstances, a secure tenant may have the right to be granted a 'shared ownership lease'. The idea of the scheme is that, where the tenant cannot afford to buy his home outright, he can instead buy a slice of a long lease with the right to go on buying further slices of the long lease until eventually he owns it outright. At that point, he can acquire the freehold, provided that the dwelling in question is a house and the landlord owns the freehold interest. In the meantime, the rent that the tenant has to pay to the landlord is reduced according to the size of the slice of the shared ownership lease he has so far bought.

In the first place, the tenant must purchase at least a 50% share in the lease. If he prefers, he may buy a larger share, which must be a multiple of 12.5%. Therefore, he may begin with 50%, 62.5%, 75% or 87.5%. He may subsequently purchase further 12.5% shares until he reaches 100%.

The right to a shared ownership lease arises where:
○ the tenant's right to buy has been established and his notice claiming to exercise it remains in force
○ the tenant has claimed the right to a mortgage but he is not entitled to a 100% advance
○ the tenant is entitled to defer completion (this means that he must pay a £100 deposit).

The Housing Act 1985 sets out the procedure to be followed when claiming a shared ownership lease. It is begun by the tenant serving a notice on the landlord; the landlord must reply within four weeks, either admitting the tenant's claim or rejecting it with reasons. Once the right to the shared ownership lease is established, the Act contains further provisions dealing with the mechanics of completing the transaction.

the price

There is a formula (shown at the top of page 202) for working out the price to be paid for the tenant's initial purchase and for calculating the discount to which he is entitled.

The Housing Act 1985 contains provisions dealing with the calculation of the rent payable by the tenant under a shared ownership lease, and the price to be paid when purchasing further slices of the lease.

A tenant claiming a shared ownership lease is entitled to a mortgage to finance the purchase, according to the rules already explained.

The initial contribution is determined by the formula

$$C = \frac{S(V - D)}{100}$$

the effective discount is determined by the formula

$$E = \frac{S \times D}{100}$$

where

C = the tenant's initial contribution

E = the effective discount

S = the tenant's initial share expressed as a percentage

V = the value of the dwelling-house at the relevant time

D = the discount to which the tenant would be entitled if he were exercising the right to buy.

if the tenant gets into difficulties

It is not inconceivable that a tenant who exercises his right to buy by acquiring a shared ownership lease might get into financial difficulties. In such a situation, the most attractive proposition from the point of view of the tenant would be for the landlord to buy back the tenant's slice, thereby enabling the tenant to become a secure tenant again. (In the process of acquiring 'slices' in a shared ownership lease, the occupier ceases to be a secure tenant.) There is, however, no provision in the Housing Act 1985 for the repurchase of shared owner-ship leases by the landlord in cases of financial hardship.

The courts have held that not only are local authority landlords not required to buy back the tenant's shared owner-ship lease, they are not even required to accept a surrender of the shared ownership lease by the tenant. Accordingly, if the tenant cannot keep up the payments of rent and mortgage instalments, the only solution is to try to sell the lease to a third party. The problem would then be that the tenant may not be entitled to be rehoused by the local authority (under its duty to house the homeless), since he may be regarded as voluntarily homeless.

THE TRANSFER OF COUNCIL HOUSING TO THE PRIVATE SECTOR

The right to buy (discussed in the previous chapter) is not the only mechanism whereby council houses and flats may be transferred into the private sector. In recent years, government policy has been to encourage the transfer of public sector housing to private sector landlords. The result of such a policy is to reduce the number of secure tenants and to increase the number of private sector tenants (either protected tenants under the Rent Act 1977 or assured tenants under the Housing Act 1988).

The policy of privatizing council housing has been put into operation in a number of phases. The Housing Act 1985 provides for the voluntary transfer of public sector housing to private landlords with the consent of the Secretary of State. The housing that may be transferred in this way may be either with vacant possession, or with sitting tenants. The transfer of council housing with secure tenants in occupation was greatly facilitated by the procedure introduced by the Housing and Planning Act 1986.

The sale of council housing to private landlords has been given further impetus by Part IV of the Housing Act 1988. The 1988 Act introduces a procedure whereby certain private institutions which are approved by the Secretary of State may apply to take over areas of council housing. If the tenants do not vote against acquisition by the private landlord, transfer may take place against the wishes of the local authority. Whereas the procedure of the Housing and Planning Act 1986 is a voluntary one, the Housing Act 1988 introduces a form of compulsory acquisition.

Since the effect of the transfer of council housing into the private sector is to deprive public sector tenants of their 'secure' status and thus of the rights of secure tenants, the seriousness of the implications of transfer are not to be underestimated. However, the law provides that in certain circumstances the transfer of public housing to a private sector landlord does not extinguish the tenant's right to buy. The Housing Act 1985 (as amended) provides that many former secure tenants will continue to enjoy what is called the 'preserved right to buy'.

voluntary transfer by local authorities

By virtue of section 32 of the Housing Act 1985, local authorities may – with the consent of the Secretary of State - dispose of land (which includes buildings) which is held for housing purposes.

Where a local authority intends to transfer dwellings which are subject to secure tenancies, not only is the consent of the Secretary of State required, but the local authority must comply with procedures laid down in section 106A and Schedule 3A of the Housing Act 1985. (These provisions were added by the Housing and Planning Act 1986.) The basic scheme of the procedure is that where the local authority seeks to dispose of some of its housing stock (with the consequence that secure tenants would become tenants of private sector landlords) the tenants must be consulted.

procedural steps

The local authority must serve a notice in writing on each of the secure tenants who will be affected by the transfer. There is no need to serve a notice on tenants who are expected to have vacated the premises before the proposed disposal. The notice should

○ inform the tenants of the details of the transfer and identity

of the person to whom it is proposed that the transfer will be made
- inform the tenants of the likely consequences of the transfer
- inform the tenants of the preserved right to buy
- specify a period of time in which the tenants may make representations to the local authority.

The local authority must consider the representations of the tenants and serve another written notice on the tenants, informing them of any relevant changes to the proposed transfer and of their right to communicate their objections to the Secretary of State. The tenants must be told that the Secretary of State must refuse to give consent to the transfer if a majority of the tenants affected oppose it.

the Secretary of State's consent
The Secretary of State may require the local authority to carry out further consultation. In any event, when the local authority has complied with the procedure and any further process of consultation as directed, the Secretary of State may then consider whether or not to give consent to the transfer. He must not give his consent to the transfer if it appears that a majority of the tenants do not want the transfer to go ahead. However, the Secretary of State has a general discretion to refuse to give consent to the transfer for other reasons (such as the identity of the landlord).

housing action trusts
The Housing Act 1988 provides for the creation of housing action trusts. Tenants of housing action trusts will be secure tenants under the Housing Act 1985.

Under section 84 of the Housing Act 1988, a housing action trust may dispose of property occupied by secure tenants, with the consent of the Secretary of State. Before the Secretary of State may consent to the transfer, the housing action trust must comply with the procedure laid down in section 84 of the 1988 Act. This procedure is very similar to that introduced by the Housing and Planning Act 1986 (described above).

transfer under the Housing Act 1988: tenants' choice

Part IV of the Housing Act 1988 contains provisions conferring on 'approved persons', including tenants' co-operatives, the right to acquire from public sector landlords the freehold of housing currently let to secure tenants. Secure tenants are given the choice whether to allow the acquisition to go ahead and, if it does, whether to transfer their tenancies into the private sector or to remain tenants of their existing public sector landlord. Tenants who decide to transfer will become assured tenants under the Housing Act 1988, and most will retain their right to buy.

Part IV of the Housing Act 1988, commonly referred to as 'tenants' choice' came into force in the spring of 1989.

approved persons

Only applicants approved by the Housing Corporation may acquire tenanted property from public sector landlords under 'tenants' choice'. The following bodies are not eligible for approval:

- a local housing authority, new town corporation, housing action trust, or the Development Board for Rural Wales
- a county council
- any other body thought by the Housing Corporation not to be independent of a public sector landlord or county council.

Apart from the above, any incorporated or unincorporated body or individual or group of individuals is eligible for approval. Applications must be accompanied by a fee, and approval may be conditional upon the applicant entering into certain undertakings with the Corporation. Very generally speaking, approval will only be given to those applicants who

are financially sound, have the expertise and resources necessary to cope with the management, maintenance and repair of
the housing they wish to acquire and who will not seek to
exploit tenants. Tenants' choice landlords will be expected,
amongst other things, to provide accommodation for those
who are inadequately housed or homeless, to pay special
attention to the housing problems of particular groups, including ethnic minorities, and to retain their housing stock for
letting at affordable rents and, except in cases of exempt
disposals (for example, where a former secure tenant exercises
his preserved right to buy), to dispose of it only with the
consent of the Secretary of State.

An application for approval takes about eight to twelve
weeks to process.

The activities of tenants' choice landlords are to be moni-
tored by the Housing Corporation which is given the power to
revoke approval in appropriate cases.

housing to be acquired

Only freehold buildings currently occupied by qualifying
tenants and other freehold property reasonably necessary for
its use, can be acquired from a public sector landlord.
Qualifying tenants are secure tenants who have the right to
buy and are not subject to a court order for possession. Some
secure tenants do not have the right to buy because, for
example, they are undischarged bankrupts.

Certain types of building cannot be acquired in any event.
These include a building

○ where more than fifty per cent of the internal floor space is,
  or will be, occupied for business purposes
○ of which currently more than half the secure tenant occupiers are not qualifiying tenants
○ which is a house currently occupied by a secure tenant who

is not a qualifying tenant or by a tenant who is not a secure tenant.

The relevant date for ascertaining the above information is the date on which the application to acquire is served on the public sector landlord concerned.

application to acquire

Once approval has been given by the Housing Corporation, a possible tenants' choice landlord can make an application to the public sector landlord concerned, specifying the buildings and other property he wishes to acquire. The application must be in the prescribed form and be accompanied by a plan.

During the next twenty weeks or so, the details of the possible acquisition, such as the property to be included and the price to be paid, are sorted out. (Any dispute is settled by binding arbitration.) At this stage, the applicant will be supplied by the public sector landlord with details of every tenant or licensee and the nature of his tenancy or licence, what repairs or improvements are necessary and the cost, how much rent is owed and by whom, and so on – in short, he will be given all the information he needs in order to pursue his application to acquire. This information is, however, confidential and the possible landlord cannot pass it on to anyone outside the proposed sale. He will also be given an opportunity to inspect those parts of the property which are not tenanted.

consultation

The next stage is for the possible landlord to consult with the tenants. He must write to them all individually explaining in detail the following:

○ his policy and procedures for selecting tenants and dealing with transfer requests

○ the terms of the tenancy he is proposing to offer
○ how he proposes to fix, and to keep under review, rent and other charges
○ repair and maintenance obligations and the procedure for carrying them out
○ his arrangements for tenant consultation and involvement in the general running and maintenance of the property as a whole
○ how he intends to deal with tenants' complaints, either against him or against other tenants
○ tenant compensation for failure of services, etc. provided by him
○ the circumstances in which the tenant may be required to move to alternative accommodation
○ his policy and the procedure for recovering arrears of rent and service charges
○ arrangements for access to personal information held by him
○ any special arrangements he might have for providing special facilities for the disabled.

This, in effect, constitutes an offer by the possible landlord to the tenants: he will not be able to renege on his bargain if the acquisition goes through.

Former secure tenants of flats, who have exercised their right to buy and have been granted long leases are entitled to be included in the consultation process (even though they are not qualifying tenants), since if the transfer goes ahead they will inevitably be affected. They are not, however, entitled to vote on whether the transfer should go ahead. If it does, they remain long-term tenants of their existing public sector landlord.

terms of the tenancy

A tenants' choice landlord can only offer (and eventually grant) his potential tenants, an assured tenancy (this should in most cases be a periodic assured tenancy). An assured short-hold tenancy is not considered to be appropriate. For an existing secure tenant of a public sector landlord, this will mean, amongst other things, three important changes:

○ The grounds upon which the landlord can seek a court order for possession are those set out in Schedule 2 to the Housing Act 1988 (discussed in detail earlier in the book) except ground 6 – redevelopment.

○ When the tenant dies, his or her spouse or common law wife or husband may succeed to the tenancy, but no such statutory right to succeed is available to other members of the tenant's family. A tenants' choice landlord may, at his discretion, allow wider succession rights. If this is to be the landlord's policy, he should inform the tenants at the consultation stage.

○ The initial rent is a matter for agreement between the landlord and the tenant. Thereafter, the landlord can in-crease the rent periodically, although there is a procedure whereby the tenant can refer such an increase to a rent assessment committee.

Some of the other rights enjoyed by secure tenants may be affected.

The right to buy is, generally speaking, preserved for former secure tenants. The right to buy is not, however, available to a new tenant who is granted an assured tenancy after the acquisition has taken place.

Tenants' choice landlords are encouraged to grant their tenants the right to exchange their accommodation with tenants of other tenants' choice landlords, registered housing authorities and local housing authorities, but they are not required by law to do so.

Similarly, landlords are encouraged, but not required, to grant their tenants the right to take in lodgers, to carry out improvements and to carry out repairs and have the cost refunded, where the landlord has failed to perform his repair-ing obligations.

A tenant's right to be consulted should not be altered significantly.

It is to be hoped that one effect of transfer will be that the standard of the tenant's accommodation will improve.

the vote

When the consultation process is over, the qualifying tenants vote on the offer that has been made to them by the possible landlord. The vote is conducted by an independent body or teller. Each tenant is sent a ballot paper, and a freepost return envelope, together with an explanation of the ballot. (Joint tenants get one ballot paper because they have one vote between them.)

The ballot paper must be returned within three weeks. During the following three weeks, however, the teller will contact those who have not voted or who have spoilt their vote, and help them to cast a valid vote.

The votes are then counted. The proposed transfer can only go ahead if

○ at least fifty per cent of the qualifying tenants have voted and
○ of those who have voted, less than fifty per cent voted to stay with their existing public sector landlord.

It is important for tenants to realise that if they do not vote and the result of the ballot is that the acquisition should go ahead, they are deemed to have voted in favour of transfer.

notice of intention to proceed and duty to complete
If the majority of the tenants are in favour, the next step is for the tenants' choice landlord to serve notice of intention to proceed on the public sector landlord.

The latter must then convey the freehold in the property to the new landlord. The freeholds of the houses of tenants who have voted 'no' to the transfer are excluded from the conveyance and remain with the public sector landlord. In the case of a block of flats, the freehold of the whole block (excluding flats occupied by non-qualifying tenants) is transferred to the tenants' choice landlord, but he is under a duty to grant a lease back to the public sector landlord of the flats of those tenants who voted against transfer. The net result is the same: tenants of houses or flats who vote 'no' remain secure tenants of the old landlord.

the preserved right to buy

When council housing is transferred from a local authority under section 32 of the Housing Act 1985 or Part IV of the Housing Act 1988, public sector tenants will cease to be secure tenants under the Housing Act 1985. It is provided, however, by sections 171A to 171H of the Housing Act 1985 (as amended) that although tenants will lose their secure status, they will not necessarily lose the right to buy. Under the 'preserved right to buy', a former secure tenant may acquire the landlord's interest after the transfer of the property from the public sector to a private landlord.

whose right is preserved?
The preserved right to buy will exist where a 'qualifying person' ceases to be a secure tenant by virtue of the transfer of the property to a private landlord. The qualifying person may be any of the following:

○ the person who was a secure tenant before the disposal to a private sector landlord
○ where the former secure tenancy was granted to joint tenants, one of the joint tenants
○ a person who on the death of the former secure tenant inherits the new tenancy
○ a person who becomes the tenant in place of the former

secure tenant by an order of the court on the breakdown of marriage.

Where a qualifying person who has the preserved right to buy subsequently becomes the tenant of other premises owned by the same landlord (or where the landlord is a company, or connected company) the tenant may exercise the preserved right to buy in relation to the new premises.

exclusions

The preserved right to buy does not arise

○ where the former landlord was a quasi-public sector body against whom the right to buy was not exercisable (such as charities and certain housing associations) or

○ in any other case provided for by the Secretary of State.

protecting the preserved right to buy by registration

In order to be able to exercise the preserved right to buy, two conditions must be satisfied. The first is that the qualifying person must continue to occupy the premises to which the right to buy relates as his only or principal home. If the former secure tenant sub-lets the premises and moves into separate accommodation, the preserved right to buy will be lost.

Secondly, the preserved right to buy is an interest which has to be protected by registration under the Land Registration Act 1925. This is provided by Schedule 9A to the Housing Act 1985. The public sector landlord which is disposing of the relevant property is required to ensure that the Chief Land Registrar is informed of those properties in relation to which the preserved right to buy exists. When the land is transferred to the new private landlord, the tenant's preserved right to buy will be protected by an entry on the register. Accordingly, it will continue to be enforceable even if the new landlord subsequently disposes of the freehold.

losing the preserved right to buy

The former secure tenant (who after transfer to the private sector landlord becomes either a protected tenant under the Rent Act 1977 or an assured tenant under the Housing Act 1988) will lose the preserved right to buy in certain circumstances.

failure to register
Where the landlord disposes of his interest, the preserved right to buy will be lost if it is not properly registered. Since it is the responsibility of the public sector landlord to ensure that the right to buy is registered, the tenant may sue the former landlord for breach of statutory duty if the preserved right to buy is lost as a result of the former landlord's default.

transfer back to the public sector
Where premises, which were transferred to the private sector, are subsequently transferred by the landlord to a public sector landlord (as defined by section 80 of the Housing Act 1980), the tenant once again becomes a secure tenant and the preserved right to buy is lost. After transfer back to the public sector, generally speaking, the tenant will once again enjoy the right to buy. Periods during which the tenant enjoyed the preserved right to buy will count towards the qualification to exercise the right to buy.

repossession and suitable alternative accommodation

Under the Rent Act 1977 and the Housing Act 1988 a landlord may apply to the court for an order of possession against a tenant on the basis that suitable alternative accommodation is available. This is a discretionary ground for possession; that is to say, the court will not order possession unless it considers it reasonable to do so.

However, it is provided that where the preserved right to buy applies, the court should not make an order for possession of the relevant premises on the basis of the availability of suitable alternative accommodation unless it is satisfied:

- that the preserved right to buy will continue to be exercisable in relation to the alternative premises (either because the landlord is the same, or an associated company), or
- that the tenant will become a secure tenant of the alternative premises (because the landlord is a public sector body within section 80 of the 1985 Act).

HOUSING BENEFIT

A tenant of a private or public sector landlord may be eligible to get housing benefit if he has an appropriately low income. Entitlement to this benefit does not depend on having paid National Insurance contributions. So even someone who gets no other social security benefits may still be eligible for housing benefit. But it is means-tested with a capital limit of £8,000 (that means that anyone who has savings or investments of more than £8,000 will not be able to get housing benefit).

The local authority works out how much housing benefit will be paid to a person who is eligible. The maximum you can get is 100% of your 'eligible rent' (this may not be the same as the amount you pay your landlord) and 80% of your 'eligible rates' (this is the amount of your rates after any rate relief, say for a disability, has been deducted).

If you have more money coming in than the allowances and premiums you qualify for (the money you need to live on, according to official calculations) you get less housing benefit. The local authority, in order to assess the level of benefit, requests the claimant to complete a very detailed form and it is advisable to do so as fully as possible, in order to avoid delay. As well as personal details, you will have to provide information on the type of letting, whether the accommodation is a house, semi-detached, flat, etc, the number of rooms and their position (ground floor, first floor, etc), the repairing obligations (that is, who is responsible for the external and/or internal decorations), the number of occupants. Anyone who has difficulty in completing the form should get advice from a citizens advice bureau or housing advice centre.

The local authority refers the completed form to the rent officer if it is a new style assured tenancy or new style assured shorthold tenancy, and some other types of lettings; the claim is not referred via the rent officer where it concerns an existing regulated tenancy or restricted contract. The rent officer has to decide (within five working days or as quickly as possible) whether the rent payable under the tenancy is reasonable – namely whether it is a market rent not higher than that paid by tenants of similar premises who are not claiming housing benefit – and whether the accommodation is appropriate for the claimant in terms of size and cost.

If the rent payable under the tenancy is considered too high, the rent officer will carry out a valuation (within twenty working days) to assess a reasonable rent for the accommodation. This may involve an inspection of the property if considered necessary. This decision as to rent will be used for housing benefit purposes.

unreasonably large accommodation
A claimant may be notified that he is deemed to be occupying unreasonably large accommodation, for example where a single person is occupying a three-bedroomed house. If the claimant is still occupying that accommodation after six months, the housing benefit will be restricted to an amount payable for accommodation of a size deemed to be appropriate for the claimant's needs of a similar type and in the same location.

unreasonably expensive accommodation
This generally applies where a claimant has moved to an expensive area. In assessing whether the accommodation is unreasonably expensive the rent officer has regard, however, to the tenant's personal needs as well as the level of open market rents in the local authority's area.

appeal

There is no appeal as such from the local authority's decision as to the amount of housing benefit awarded.

An aggrieved claimant can nevertheless complain to the

local authority, who should consider the complaint and try to resolve the matter. If the complaint concerns the decision as to the rent level for the property (it may of course concern other matters, such as personal circumstances), the local authority may refer the matter back to the rent officer service. A review by two or three experienced rent officers (possibly involving one or more from outside the area) may be undertaken and their decision notified to the local authority. Challenging this decision would be by way of judicial review.

OBLIGATIONS AND REMEDIES

The relationship of landlord and tenant necessarily involves rights and obligations between the parties. Where the parties have entered a written agreement, the terms of the lease itself will impose a number of obligations (express covenants) on each of the parties.

However, not all obligations between landlord and tenant are created in this way. A written lease may be silent on certain important points, or a tenancy may arise by virtue of an oral agreement, in which case there will be no written terms. In these situations, the law implies obligations between the parties (implied covenants). Some obligations are imposed by statute so that the parties cannot contract out of them.

Here follows a description of the most significant obligations which the landlord owes to the tenant and the various remedies which are available to tenants when the landlord is in breach of his obligations.

repairs

Both the landlord and the tenant may be faced with express repairing covenants as well as implied obligations.

express obligations

A lease often contains a covenant expressly allocating responsibility for repair and maintenance. It is not uncommon – especially in a lease of short duration, such as a periodic tenancy – for responsibility for repairs to be shared between the landlord and the tenant. A lease may stipulate that the landlord is responsible for the upkeep of the structure and exterior of the premises, and that the tenant is liable for internal repairs. In relation to long leases (such as for 99 years) at a low rent, it is not uncommon for the tenant to be made liable for all repairs.

The extent of any express repairing obligation depends on the precise words used. A lease may impose an obligation on the tenant 'to put and keep in repair', or 'to keep in repair', or simply 'to repair', or 'to repair, fair wear and tear excepted'.

Each of these phrases has a different legal significance. A tenant who covenants 'to keep in repair' or 'to put and keep the premises in repair' is responsible for remedying any disrepair which exists at the time when the lease is granted. A covenant in this form is unusual in short-term lettings. If, on the other hand, the covenant simply requires the tenant 'to repair the premises', the tenant is only required to remedy defects which arise during the course of the tenancy.

fair wear and tear excepted
If a repairing covenant includes the phrase 'fair wear and tear excepted' the tenant is exempted from having to remedy defects which arise through the passage of time, through reasonable use by the tenant or as a result of natural forces. Also, the tenant will not be liable for the gradual deterioration in the state of internal decorations, furniture or carpets. However, the tenant may be responsible for the damage which is a consequence of disrepair normally regarded as within the 'fair wear and tear' exception. For example, if a tile falls off the roof in a storm, and as a result rain-water causes damage to the interior of the premises, the tenant will be liable for the internal disrepair, even though he would not be responsible for the original defect (which was the result of the operation of natural forces).

implied obligations

Although leases often include express repairing covenants (especially covenants imposing obligations on the tenant to maintain the interior of the premises), it is quite possible for a lease not to address the issue of the repairing obligations of the parties. This will almost inevitably be the case in relation to a periodic or short fixed term tenancy which has been created by oral agreement rather than in writing. However, the absence of express repairing covenants does not mean that the parties to the lease are free from responsibility for repairs.

A periodic tenant is under a general duty to keep the premises 'in a tenant-like manner'. This requires the tenant to take proper care of the place. It was said in one case that the tenant "must, if he is going away for the winter, turn off the water and empty the boiler. He must get the chimneys cleaned, when necessary, and also clean the windows. He must get the electric light mended when it fuses. He must unstop the sink when it is blocked by his waste . . . But apart from such things, if the house falls into disrepair through fair wear and tear or lapse of time, or for any reason not caused by him, then the tenant is not liable to repair it."

The landlord's position is rather different. In a wide variety of circumstances, the law implies into a tenancy (including a tenancy created orally) covenants requiring the landlord to undertake action to ensure that the environmental quality of rented accommodation is of a suitable standard. There are two aspects: fitness for human habitation and repairs.

fitness for human habitation

From the tenant's point of view, the law is unsatisfactory in the sense that there is no general duty on a landlord to ensure that rented premises are fit for human habitation. There are, however, two minor exceptions.

According to an old common law rule, a landlord who lets furnished premises impliedly guarantees that the premises are fit for human habitation at the date of the letting. Accordingly, if the premises are unfit for human habitation – for example, as a result of being infested with bugs, or because the lavatory does not work – the tenant can reject the tenancy and claim damages for any loss which he has suffered. This rule is however of very limited value to the tenant for a number of reasons:

○ the tenant cannot require the landlord to make the premises fit for human habitation; his only remedy is to terminate the tenancy and claim damages
○ the rule has no application where the premises are fit for human habitation when let, but become unfit for human habitation at some subsequent point during the tenancy
○ the rule relates only to unfitness for human habitation, and not to disrepair generally
○ the rule applies only to furnished lettings.

Under section 8 of the Landlord and Tenant Act 1985, where a house or part of a house is let at a low rent, there is an implied condition by the landlord that the house is fit for human habitation at the beginning of the tenancy and an implied undertaking by the landlord that he will keep the premises fit for human habitation throughout the term. The scope of this provision is severely limited, to the point of being effectively nullified, by the fact that the section only applies to premises let at an annual rent of £80 in London, and £52 elsewhere.

repairs
In relation to repairs, the law provides the tenant with more effective protection. However, the law is very complex. Different rules apply to different categories of tenancy depending on the date of their creation.

– tenancies created on or after 24 October 1961
In practical terms perhaps the most important of the implied obligations is to be found in section 11 of the Landlord and Tenant Act 1985 (formerly section 32 of the Housing Act 1961).

Where a lease was created for a term of less than seven years, the landlord is under an obligation

○ to keep in repair the structure and exterior of the premises
○ to keep in repair and in proper working order the installations for the supply of water, gas and electricity and for sanitation
○ to keep in repair and proper working order the installations for space heating and heating water.

The obligations which this section establishes are absolute, in the sense that the landlord cannot escape liability simply by showing that he took reasonable steps to keep the premises and installations in repair. Furthermore, the landlord cannot contract out of these responsibilities: a clause in the tenancy requiring the tenant to perform these tasks would be of no effect.

The 'structure and exterior' includes: the main fabric of the building (such as the external walls and the roof); a partition wall between the tenant's premises and another dwelling; the path and steps which are the ordinary means of access to a house; wall plaster and rendering; woodwork; skylights and windows. In relation to a flat, the 'structure and exterior' extends to the outside walls of the flat, the outside of the inner party wall of the flat, the outer sides of the horizontal divisions between the flat and the flats above and below, and the ceilings and wall of the flat.

The term 'installations' includes gas and water pipes, electrical wiring, water tanks, lavatory cisterns, boilers, radiators, and other forms of heating installation. An installation may have to be replaced by the landlord under the obligation created by section 11 if it is not in proper working order because of a design fault.

To fall within the scope of the repairing obligation implied by section 11, the installation in question must be located in the premises occupied by the tenant. This limitation may present problems for tenants of flats in tower-blocks or houses on large council estates. It is not uncommon for the landlord to provide heating for a large number of the residents by means of a single central heating boiler. In these circumstances, the tenant has no recourse against the landlord under section 11 if the boiler breaks down.

Section 11 as originally drafted left a certain number of gaps. Particular problems have arisen in relation to the common parts (such as staircases) of buildings in multiple occupation and communal facilities (such as lifts). On occasion the courts have implied into the contractual relationship between the landlord and the tenant an obligation requiring the landlord to undertake certain repairs. In one case concerning a tower-block divided into separate dwellings it was held that the landlord was under an implied contractual duty to take reasonable steps to ensure that the common parts were properly maintained and that the lifts were in proper working order. (The agreement which the tenant had signed made no mention at all of the landlord's repairing obligations.) The landlord's implied obligation was not regarded by the court to be an absolute one, but merely an obligation to take reasonable steps. Therefore it did not automatically follow from the fact that the common parts were in a deplorable state, and that the lifts were repeatedly out of order, that the landlord was in breach of his obligation. On the facts, it was held that the tenant had not established that the landlord had failed to take reasonable care.

– tenancies created on or after 15 January 1989
The Housing Act 1988 has resolved some of the problems described above by rendering the landlord's repairing obligations under section 11 more onerous. However, this applies only in relation to leases entered into after the coming into force of the Act.

First, the landlord's obligation to keep the structure and exterior of the premises in repair is extended to 'any part of the building in which the lessor has an estate or interest'. This means that where a building is divided into separate units of living accommodation, the landlord has an obligation to keep the common parts (staircases etc.) in repair.

Secondly, the landlord's obligation to keep installations (for the supply of water, sanitation, heating etc.) in proper working order is extended to any installation which serves the premises occupied by the tenant as long as the installation either forms part of any building owned by the landlord, or is owned by the landlord or is under his control.

These obligations are qualified in two ways:

○ the landlord is required to carry out the extended repairs only if the disrepair to the building or the failure to maintain the installations in proper working order is of such a nature that it affects the tenant's enjoyment of the premises or the common parts

○ in cases where, in order to carry out repair work, the landlord requires access to a part of the building to which he does not enjoy a right of access, the landlord is not liable for the disrepair if he uses all reasonable endeavours to obtain the necessary rights of access which would enable him to carry out the repairs, but is unable to do so.

– tenancies created before 24 October 1961

In relation to leases created before 24 October 1961, there are no repairing obligations imposed by statute. However, the courts will, in certain circumstances, be prepared to imply a repairing obligation into the tenancy. In a recent case, concerning a periodic tenancy which had been created in 1941, the lease contained a provision which made the tenant liable for internal repairs. There was no provision allocating responsibility for external repairs. The court was of the view that the covenant imposed on the tenant could not be properly carried out unless the exterior of the premises was kept in repair. Accordingly, in order to give business efficacy to the lease, the court implied into the tenancy an obligation on the landlord to keep the exterior and structure of the premises in repair.

the meaning of 'repair'

The meaning which the law attaches to the word 'repair' is clearly of prime importance, since defects, however important they may be, which are not within the legal definition of 'repair' will fall outside the scope of repairing obligations arising under express or implied covenants.

The problems which a tenant might face in making a landlord liable for defects in the premises are revealed in a case decided in 1985 (*Quick v Taff-Ely BC*). The tenant of a council house complained to the local authority that the house suffered from extreme dampness as a result of condensation. The cause of the condensation was the design of the windows. Although the effect of the dampness was to cause damage to the internal decoration, and the tenant's bedding, furniture and clothes, the landlord was not found liable. The tenant could not point to any part of the structure or exterior of the premises which required repair.

However, extensive remedial work may fall within the scope of a repairing obligation (whether express or implied), notwithstanding the fact that the problem stems from an 'inherent fault' or a 'design defect'. It is an essential (but not sufficient) precondition that the tenant establishes that there is some part of the exterior or structure which is damaged. Once this is done, if the damage is 'caused by an unsuspected inherent defect then it may be necessary to cure the defect, and thus to some extent improve without wholly renewing the property as the only practicable way of making good the damage to the subject matter of the repairing covenant.'

The standard of repair which will be required depends on the nature of the property in question. A landlord will not be required under a repairing covenant to bring an old property up to modern standards. In determining the standard of repair required it is necessary to have regard to the age, character, and prospective life of the property, and to the locality in which it is situated. So, in one case it was held a local authority landlord was not required to insert a damp proof course into a run-down back-to-back terraced house built early this century even though the house was subject to extreme damp.

inspection, access and notice

Where the tenant covenants to keep the premises in repair, the landlord will normally reserve the right to inspect the premises. Where the landlord is under an obligation to carry out repairs, he will have (either under statute or at common law) a right of access in order to inspect the premises, and to carry out any necessary repairs. The only qualification to this right is that the landlord must give the tenant reasonable notice.

The landlord is only liable (under either an express or implied covenant) in respect of disrepair of which he has knowledge. Where disrepair is not apparent to either the landlord or the tenant – because it is undetectable by superficial inspection – this may result in hardship to the tenant. In one case the tenant was injured when the bedroom ceiling collapsed. Some years previously the occupiers of the flat above had caused violent vibrations by frequent and prolonged dancing and banging on the floor. No defect in the ceiling was visible. It was held that the landlord was not liable, since he had no knowledge or notice of the fact that the ceiling was defective.

tell the landlord

Since a landlord becomes liable for latent and invisible defects only when they become patent and brought to the landlord's knowledge, it is extremely important that the tenant should take steps to inform the landlord in the event of the premises falling into a state of disrepair. Notice does not have to be given in a particular form. A letter sent to the landlord setting out the nature of the disrepair is sufficient. In certain circumstances, the landlord will be deemed to have had notice of disrepair through an agent (such as a rent-collector, a workman or a caretaker).

other obligations under the general law

The general law imposes obligations on the owners of property: under the Occupier's Liability Act 1957 a landlord who retains part of a building under his control owes a duty to take such care as is reasonable, to see that tenants and visitors will be reasonably safe in using the premises. The Occupier's Liability Act 1984 imposes a similar duty towards trespassers and those entering the premises under a contract (such as service engineers and workmen). The Defective Premises Act 1972 provides that if the landlord is under an obligation to repair, or has a right to repair, he owes a duty to anyone who might reasonably be affected by lack of repair.

what the landlord can do

If the tenant is in breach of his obligations to carry out repairs, the landlord will normally try and get the tenant to comply with his obligations and will require him to pay compensation for any loss which the landlord may have suffered. The landlord is not allowed to recover a greater amount than that by which the value of the landlord's interest has decreased as a result of the tenant's breach of the repairing covenant.

The only effective alternative is for the landlord to bring proceedings with a view to terminating the tenancy and getting back possession. Where a tenant has failed to keep the premises in repair, the landlord may seek repossession under ground 12 in relation to assured tenancies under the Housing Act 1988, under case 1 in relation to tenancies falling within the Rent Act 1977, and under ground 1 in relation to secure tenancies falling within the Housing Act 1985. In each of these situations the tenant's default gives rise to only a discretionary ground for possession. So the court will only grant an order for possession if it is satisfied that it is reasonable to do so.

what the tenant can do

The tenant's remedies for the landlord's failure to comply with his repairing obligations can be broken down into two categories: civil remedies (which require private action on the part of the tenant) and public law remedies (whereby the tenant seeks to enlist the support of the local authority).

civil remedies

For the purposes of the discussion which follows it is assumed that the following conditions are satisfied:

- the landlord is liable to carry out certain repairs (according to the principles outlined above)
- the tenant has notified the landlord of the disrepair
- the landlord has failed to carry out the necessary repairs within a reasonable period.

From the tenant's point of view, the most attractive remedies would involve self-help, in particular withholding rent or using rent to pay for repairs etc., since, in relative terms, these remedies involve less expense than litigation. While there are circumstances in which tenants may withhold rent, it should be emphasised that as a general rule tenants are not entitled to withhold rent on the ground that the landlord is in breach of his obligations. Self-help remedies should be used with extreme caution. If they are used improperly, the tenant runs the risk that the landlord will be able to recover possession on the ground of the tenant's failure to pay rent.

doing the repairs

Under certain strict conditions, a tenant may carry out repairs which the landlord has failed to undertake and recover the costs from future rent. In order to ensure that the landlord cannot claim that he has acted improperly, the tenant who wishes to rely on this should take the steps of:

○ warning the landlord of what he proposes to do
○ giving the landlord adequate time to carry out the repairs
○ obtaining estimates for the proposed work and selecting the contractor who has given the lowest estimate
○ submitting an invoice to the landlord requesting reimbursement
○ deducting the cost from future rent only if the landlord refuses to reimburse the costs.

The tenant can only recoup the costs of the repairs by this procedure. Any damages which the tenant may have suffered (such as damage to furniture and bedding as a result of damp) cannot be recovered in this way.

secure tenants' right to repair

Since 1 January 1986 secure tenants (with the exception of tenants of co-operative housing associations) have been able to employ a special statutory procedure – established by the Secure Tenancies (Right to Repair Scheme) Regulations 1985, SI 85/1493 - enabling rent to be used to pay for certain repairs.

The scheme is limited to 'qualifying repairs' which means any repairs for which the landlord is responsible other than repairs to the structure and exterior of a flat. Under the scheme, the tenant must begin by serving a notice on the landlord describing the proposed works, why they are needed and the materials to be used. The landlord must then reply within 21 days either granting or refusing the tenant's repair claim.

The landlord may refuse the claim in the following circumstances:

○ where the landlord's costs would be more than £200
○ where the landlord intends to carry out the work within 28 days of the claim
○ where the works are not reasonably necessary for the personal comfort or safety of the tenant and those living with him, and the landlord intends to carry them out within one year as part of a planned programme of repair
○ where the works would infringe the terms of any guarantee of which the landlord has the benefit
○ where the tenant has unreasonably failed to provide the landlord with access to inspect the site for the works.

The landlord must refuse the claim in the following circumstances:

○ where the landlord's costs would be less than £20
○ where the works do not constitute a qualifying repair
○ where the works if carried out using the materials specified would not, in the landlord's opinion, satisfactorily remedy the lack of repair.

If the landlord accepts the claim, it must serve a notice on the tenant specifying:

○ the date by which a claim for compensation must be made following completion of the work
○ the amount that it would cost the authority to carry out the works itself
○ the percentage of those costs that it is prepared to pay; this figure must not be less than 75% and may be up to 100%
○ any modifications of the work and/or materials which it requires.

The tenant may then proceed to carry out the work in question and to make a claim to the landlord for payment. The landlord must then pay the tenant, except in a few specified circumstances (for example, that the work has not been done satisfactorily).

If the landlord refuses to reply to the tenant's notice, the tenant may serve a 'default notice' on the landlord. If he still receives no reply within seven days, he may proceed with the work and claim the cost, up to a maximum of £200, from the landlord.

Any disputes that arise may be referred by either party to the county court.

set-off

Equitable set-off is not in itself a mechanism for ensuring that the landlord undertakes repairs. Equitable set-off is in the nature of a defence against the landlord's claim for unpaid rent. The situations in which equitable set-off becomes relevant arise when:

○ the landlord has failed to comply with his repairing obligations
○ as a result of the disrepair the tenant has suffered damage to health, property etc.
○ the tenant has failed to pay rent
○ the landlord has commenced proceedings against the tenant in respect of the rent arrears.

In these circumstances the court will allow the tenant to deduct from the rent arrears the damages which the tenant has suffered as a result of the landlord's breach of the repairing obligation, such as damage to the tenant's furniture and other belongings. If the amount of damages is greater than the rent arrears, equitable set-off operates as a complete defence to the landlord's action, that is, the landlord will not get a possession order.

Where the damages amount to only a part of the rent arrears, the tenant exposes himself to an action by the landlord for repossession based on the tenant's non-payment of rent. Even if the tenant could defend a possession action successfully, he must be prepared to pay off the arrears in relation to that part of the rent for which set-off is not available.

suing the landlord

The tenant may choose to sue the landlord. The tenant's claim for disrepair is generally started by the issue of a summons in the local county court. In the normal course of events, the tenant will seek both an order of specific performance and damages. If granted, the order of specific performance will require the landlord to perform his obligations under the repairing covenant. If the landlord fails to perform the works stipulated in the order, he is punishable for contempt of court (which may take the form of a fine or, in extreme cases imprisonment).

The tenant will also normally be entitled to substantial damages. The purpose of damages is to place the tenant, as far as possible, in the position he would have been in had the landlord not been in breach of his obligations.

The tenant will be entitled to compensation for:

○ inconvenience, disappointment, discomfort, ill health and distress caused by the landlord's failure to repair the premises
○ the cost of any repairing works, as long as such expenses were reasonably incurred
○ if the premises are rendered uninhabitable as a result of the disrepair, the tenant may recover any costs reasonably incurred in taking alternative accommodation
○ damage to property as a result of the landlord's breach, including damage to furniture, curtains, carpets, and clothing destroyed by damp.

appointing a manager

The Landlord and Tenant Act 1987 provides further options for residential tenants in the private sector.

On the application of two or more tenants, the court may appoint a manager to take over the management of the premises from the landlord. The tenants must first serve a notice on the landlord specifying the defaults which justify the appointment of a manager and, if the problems can be remedied, giving the landlord reasonable time in which to take the necessary steps. If the court thinks that it would be 'just and convenient' to make an appointment, a manager may be appointed. A manager may be given full powers to collect the rent, and have repairs undertaken.

applying for a compulsory purchase order
In extreme cases, tenants may be entitled to acquire compulsorily the landlord's interest. Compulsory acquisition under the Landlord and Tenant Act 1987 is not available to periodic tenants or tenants occupying premises under short fixed-term tenancies. In order to make an application for an 'acquisition order' the tenants must be holding long leases (that is, of more than twenty-one years).

buying the landlord's interest
The law provides a number of mechanisms whereby certain categories of tenant may acquire the landlord's interest. By acquiring the landlord's interest, the tenant(s) can take over the management of the building.

public law remedies

Although civil remedies are superficially attractive, private litigation can be slow, expensive and frustrating. Except in the most clear-cut cases there is always the possibility that the tenant will be unsuccessful, or successful only in part. The county court judge may rule that a particular defect is not within the scope of the landlord's repairing obligation, or the landlord is not in breach, or the court may not accept the tenant's assessment of the extent of the damage suffered. Because of these problems and uncertainties, a tenant should in appropriate circumstances consider other remedies, such as those provided by the Public Health Act 1936, the Building Act 1984 and the Housing Act 1985.

Public Health Act 1936

The Public Health Act 1936 provides a basis for attacking the effects of bad housing conditions. In certain instances, a tenant will be able to rely on the support of the local authority and where a local authority declines to intervene, an individual tenant may himself institute proceedings under the Act.

The key to the operation of the Public Health Act 1936, in the present context, is the concept of a 'statutory nuisance'. Disrepair is not in itself a basis for proceedings under the 1936 Act, although many consequences of disrepair (such as damp and infestation by bugs) will constitute a statutory nuisance. Of those factual situations which amount to a statutory nuisance the most important is to be found in section 92(1)(a): 'any premises in such a state as to be prejudicial to health or a nuisance'.

The phrase 'prejudicial to health or a nuisance' has been considered by the courts on numerous occasions. The formula 'prejudicial to health' covers both actual and potential ill-health or injury. Premises which are likely to cause an ill person to deteriorate further will fall within section 92(1)(a). However, premises which give rise to mere discomfort are not regarded as being 'prejudicial to health'.

Within the context of section 92(1)(a) the courts have interpreted 'nuisance' in a technical and restrictive way. To fall within the scope of the section, a 'nuisance' must be either a private nuisance at common law, or a public nuisance at common law. A public nuisance is activity which adversely affects the reasonable comfort and convenience of life of a section of the community. A private nuisance is an unreasonable interference with a person's use or enjoyment of land (that is, property).

The present position with regard to the scope of section 92(1)(a) is as follows:

○ if personal discomfort results from the disrepair of adjacent property, the tenant may take action on the basis that the adjacent premises are a 'nuisance'

○ disrepair of either the premises occupied by the tenant or adjacent premises can give rise to an action on the basis of prejudice to health, but this does not extend to mere discomfort.

Matters such as a leaking lavatory, blocked pipes, drains and gutters, and noisy heating installations could all fall within the scope of section 92(1)(a).

procedure

The procedure under the 1936 Act may be initiated by the tenant bringing the existence of a statutory nuisance to the attention of the local authority. Complaints relating to housing conditions are handled by the council's environmental health officer. On receiving a complaint, he should come and inspect the premises in question. If the local authority is satisfied of the existence of a statutory nuisance, it is required to take action. The first step is the service of an 'abatement notice' on the person by whose 'act, default or sufferance' the statutory nuisance exists. This is normally the landlord. The notice requires the landlord to take remedial action necessary to put an end to the statutory nuisance.

If the landlord fails to take the remedial action in the stipulated time, the local authority is bound to commence proceedings in the magistrates' court. If it is established at the hearing that the landlord has failed to remedy the problem, the court will make a 'nuisance order', requiring the landlord to take the necessary action. The landlord may be fined for failure to comply with the nuisance order. In addition, the landlord is normally required to pay the local authority's costs.

in the magistrates' court

Although the local authority is required to act in relation to statutory nuisances, there may be delays, or the local authority may take the view that the tenant's allegation of a statutory nuisance is unfounded. (The local authority may be unwilling to accept the existence of a statutory nuisance in relation to local authority housing.) In such cases, the tenant may initiate proceedings in the magistrates' court under section 99 of the Public Health Act 1936.

Proceedings brought by the tenant under section 99 will, if successful, result in the magistrates' court making an order against the landlord or the local authority requiring action to be taken to put an end to the statutory nuisance. The magistrates' court has a wide discretion as to the precise form which the order should take. The court may order the installation of central heating, rewiring, insulation, the renewal of defective windows, etc.

Section 99 proceedings are criminal (rather than civil) and therefore the burden of proof is higher. It must be established beyond all reasonable doubt that a statutory nuisance exists. With regard to civil proceedings (for example, an action for damages arising out of an alleged breach of a repairing covenant), the plaintiff has to establish his case merely on the balance of probabilities.

Building Act 1984 – the quicker way

The procedure set out in the Public Health Act 1936 is inappropriate in situations where urgent action is required. If the local authority considers that the usual procedure for dealing with a statutory nuisance would cause unreasonable delay, it may, under section 76 of the Building Act 1984, serve the landlord with a nine-day notice, indicating the remedial work which the landlord should undertake. If, within seven days, the landlord serves a counter-notice of his intention to carry out the works, the local authority can only take action in relation to the statutory nuisance if the landlord fails to start remedial work in a reasonable time, or if remedial work is not progressing at a reasonable rate. However, if the landlord fails to serve a counter-notice, at the expiry of the nine day period stipulated in the original notice, the local authority may carry out the necessary repairs and recoup the cost and expenses from the landlord.

The procedure under the Building Act 1984 is particularly useful because tenants may be able to encourage the landlord to carry out urgent repairs quickly, under the threat of an emergency nine-day notice being served.

Housing Act 1985

The Housing Act 1985 provides tenants in the private sector with the possibility of enlisting the support of the local authority in two situations: where the premises are in a state of disrepair, or where the premises are unfit for human habitation. The procedures outlined below do not, however, apply to premises owned and controlled by the local authority.

for disrepair

Where premises are in a state of disrepair and substantial repairs are required to bring the property up to a reasonable standard, the local authority may serve a repair notice on the landlord requiring the performance of specified remedial work. An important limitation is that internal decorative repair cannot be included in the repair notice.

The landlord may appeal against the notice to the county court, which will have to consider such factors as the cost of the work and the value of the property.

If the landlord does not appeal or is not successful in his appeal and then fails to carry out the works specified in the notice, the local authority may undertake the repairs and recoup the cost from the landlord. Failure by the landlord to comply with a repairs notice is a criminal offence.

if unfit for human habitation

If housing is unfit for human habitation, the tenant may set in motion the procedure laid down in the Housing Act 1985 by making a complaint to the local authority.

The environmental health officer is then required to make an inspection of the premises. If the local authority appears to be refusing to consider whether the premises are unfit for human habitation, the tenant can request a justice of the peace to visit the premises. If the JP is of the view that the premises are unfit, he should make a complaint to the local authority, and then the local authority is required to inspect the premises.

For the purposes of the statutory procedure, there is a nine-point list of factors which must be considered to determine whether or not premises are unfit: repair, stability, freedom from damp, internal arrangement, natural lighting, ventilation, water supply, drainage and sanitation, facilities for cooking and the disposal of waste water. Factors not coming within the list (such as infestation by bugs) are to be ignored for the purposes of the Act. (Of course, in the case of infestation by bugs the tenant may seek to rely on the Public Health Act 1936.)

repair notice

Once it is established that the premises are unfit for human habitation, the local authority must serve a repair notice, unless it is satisfied that the premises cannot be rendered fit for human habitation at reasonable expense. To consider whether the expense is reasonable it is necessary to have regard to the estimated cost of the repairs, and the estimated value of the premises when the repairs are completed.

It is a criminal offence for the landlord to fail to comply with a repair notice. If he does so, the local authority may undertake work in default, but it is not under an obligation to do so and can recoup the cost from the landlord.

time-and-place notice

If it is decided that the premises cannot be made fit for human habitation at reasonable expense, the local authority will normally issue a time-and-place notice informing the landlord of the authority's intention to consider the future of the property. The notice states the time (at least 21 days after service of the notice) and the place where the future of the property will be considered. If the owner cannot be persuaded to undertake the necessary remedial work, the local authority is required to serve a demolition order, subject to two exceptions:

○ if it is impracticable to demolish the premises, the local authority can make a closing order, which necessitates the premises being vacated

○ the local authority may make a purchase order if it considers that the premises could be used for temporary accommodation.

Where, as a result of the procedure outlined above, a tenant is required to give up possession of the premises, normally he will be entitled to be rehoused, and to receive monetary compensation.

overlap

There is some overlap between the powers conferred on local authorities by the Public Health Act 1936 and the Housing Act 1985. In situations where premises are out of repair to the extent that they are both a statutory nuisance (for the purpose of the 1936 Act) and unfit for human habitation (within the meaning of the Housing Act 1985) the courts have indicated that local authorities should use the Housing Act procedure.

the unforeseen danger

However, there are also dangers. By involving the local authority under the Public Health Act 1936 or the Housing Act 1985 the tenant is running the risk that it will be decided that the premises are unfit for human habitation. At the very least this often involves the tenant having to vacate the premises in the short term while repairs are being carried out. If the premises cannot be put in repair at reasonable expense, the tenant will require rehousing on a permanent basis. Although the local authority will be under a statutory obligation to rehouse a displaced tenant, there is no guarantee that suitable permanent accommodation, will be available. There is no guarantee that a displaced tenant will not end up being offered unsatisfactory, temporary accommodation.

future legislation

There is currently before Parliament the Local Government and Housing Bill; it is likely that this will receive the royal assent during the summer of 1989. The Bill proposes a number of important changes regarding local authority powers in relation to housing which is unfit or in a state of disrepair.

Under the Housing Act 1985 local authorities are empowered to take action in relation to housing which is in bad condition (such as issuing repair notices, or making closing orders and demolition orders).

The Local Government and Housing Bill seeks to make certain changes to these powers.

service charges

In addition to rent, many tenants have to pay service charges. These service charges are normally paid to the landlord, or to a managing agent. Service charges are designed to cover the cost of certain expenditure on the building, such as repairs and insurance.

The Landlord and Tenant Act 1985 provided some measure of control over service charges. This control has been strengthened by the Landlord and Tenant Act 1987. The primary aim of the legislation is to ensure that the money received by the landlord (or his agent) is used for the purposes for which it is collected.

Service charges are limited to costs which have been reasonably incurred or are likely to be incurred in the provision of services and works. Moreover, the work must have been carried out to a reasonable standard. For works costing more than £1000 (or more than £50 per flat) two estimates must be obtained, one of which should be from a firm not connected with the landlord. Where there is a recognised tenants' association it must be consulted prior to the carrying out of the work, and tenants are entitled to be given a breakdown of the costing. Where costs have been incurred more than 18 months before a demand is made of the tenant, the costs cannot be recovered.

Service charges have to be held by the landlord or his agent in a trust fund. This means that the money collected by the levying of service charges can only be used for specific purposes, namely paying for those items of expenditure to which the service charges relate. At the end of his lease the tenant cannot, however, recover a share of the money which has been paid into the fund. The fund continues to be used for the benefit of the tenants who are for the time being occupying the building. If all the leases expire and the building becomes vacant, the landlord is entitled to any money remaining in the trust fund.

The Federation of Private Residents' Associations, 11 Dartmouth Street, London, SW1H 9BL (telephone 01-222 0037) concerns itself, amongst other things, with service charges.

tenants' rights to information

The landlord must provide a rent book where rent is payable weekly.

A rent book is useful because of the information it must

contain. Section 5 of the Landlord and Tenant Act 1985 provides that a rent book must state the name and address of the landlord and his agent, the address of the premises, the rent and rates payable by the occupier, and the terms and conditions of the tenancy.

In relation to regulated tenancies, restricted contracts, and assured tenancies, the rent book must explain the tenant's right to security of tenure, and mention the existence of the housing benefit scheme. As regards regulated tenancies and restricted contracts, the rent book should also explain the tenant's right to rent control.

Failure to provide a rent book is a criminal offence punishable by a fine, but it does not affect the landlord's right to be paid rent properly due to him.

A rent book is a convenient way of bringing to tenants' attention information about their rights, and it also provides a record of the terms of the tenancy, so reducing the possibility of disputes. The rationale behind the rule that a rent book needs to be provided only where rent is payable weekly is that weekly tenancies are hardly ever in writing; weekly tenants therefore require some form of protection as regards information.

details of the landlord

Any tenant who occupies residential accommodation is entitled under section 1 of the Landlord and Tenant Act 1985 to be supplied with the name and address of his landlord if he makes a written request to the person who collects the rent or to the person who receives the rent, or to the landlord's agent. This information must be given by the person to whom the request was made within 21 days. Failure to provide the information is a criminal offence punishable with a fine of up to £500.

Where the landlord is a company, the tenant is entitled to be given a list of the names and addresses of the directors and the secretary.

when the landlord assigns his interest

According to section 3 of the Landlord and Tenant Act 1985 a new landlord must give details of his name and address to the tenants within two months of acquiring the property. In practice, tenants will normally discover that there is a new landlord before the two months have elapsed, since the new landlord will have to produce an authority signed by the previous landlord (or his agent) indicating that the rent should be paid to the new landlord.

Until the tenants have been informed of the identity of the new landlord (either by the new landlord himself or by the previous landlord) the old landlord remains liable to the tenants on the covenants contained in the lease.

information required by the Landlord and Tenant Act 1987

These provisions do not apply to tenancies protected under Part II of the Landlord and Tenant Act 1954; this category of tenant has been dealt with under the heading *Tenancies for mixed residential and business purposes* (page 127 onwards).

demands made by the landlord

Where any written demand is given to the tenant (such as a demand for rent), the landlord's name and address must be contained in the document. If the demand does not contain this information, the tenant can ignore the demand until the information is provided by the landlord.

official address

The landlord is required to provide the tenant with an address in England and Wales at which notices (including notices in legal proceedings) may be served. If the landlord fails to comply with this obligation, any rent or other payment which would normally be payable can be validly withheld by the tenant.

searching the register

The general rule is that a person may only search the Land Registry register with the consent of the owner. As an exception to this general rule, a tenant may, if the title to the property is registered, inspect the register with a view to finding out the name and address of the landlord.

further rights of secure tenants

Under the Housing Act 1985, public sector landlords are required to publish information from time to time explaining in simple terms:

○ the express terms of its secure tenancies
○ the 'right to buy' provisions contained in the Housing Act 1985
○ the landlord's repairing obligations under the Landlord and Tenant Act 1985.

The landlord must supply its secure tenants with a copy of this information and a written statement of the terms of the tenancy in so far as they do not appear in the lease or written tenancy agreement and are not implied by law. This statement must be supplied when the tenancy is granted or as soon as practicable afterwards.

Public sector landlords must also publish a summary of their rules for determining priority between applicants for housing and for dealing with applications by secure tenants to move to other dwelling-houses let under secure tenancies. These rules must be made available for inspection at the landlord's principal office at all reasonable hours, free of charge.

Provision also exists for the Secretary of State to require landlords to give information to tenants regarding charges made for heating and the supply of hot water, where this is provided in accordance with a local scheme. As yet, the Secretary of State has not brought this provision into effect.

Finally, public sector landlords must, on request, provide their secure tenants with details of their consultation procedure.

tenant's right to quiet enjoyment

The situations in which landlords can lawfully recover possession of residential premises are strictly limited. During a period of rapidly increasing property prices, some landlords wanting to realise the capital value of their investment might be tempted to take the law into their own hands, and to pursue actions designed to encourage tenants to vacate the premises. The law provides occupiers of residential premises with a range of remedies to counteract unlawful eviction or harassment by property owners. However, the relevant rules and principles in this area are complex.

A single set of facts can both constitute a crime and give rise to civil liability. For example, if a landlord evicts a tenant without a court order, the landlord may be prosecuted (criminal law) for unlawful eviction under section 1 of the Protection from Eviction Act 1977, and may be sued (civil law) by the tenant for damages.

criminal liability

The Protection from Eviction Act 1977 (as amended by section 29 of the Housing Act 1988) creates one criminal offence of unlawful eviction and two criminal offences of harassment.

unlawful eviction
As a general proposition, it is unlawful for a landlord to evict an occupier of residential premises without a court order. However, the landlord may, on the termination of the tenancy or licence, recover possession without a court order if the

tenancy or licence was entered into on or after 15 January 1989, and it falls within one of the following situations:

○ the occupier shares any accommodation with the landlord, and the landlord occupies the premises as his only or principal home

○ the occupier shares any accommodation with a member of the landlord's family, that person occupies the premises as his only or principal home, and the landlord occupies as his only or principal home premises in the same building

○ the tenancy or licence was granted as a temporary expedient to an occupier who entered the premises as a trespasser

○ the tenancy or licence confers a right to occupy premises for a holiday

○ the tenancy or licence is rent-free

○ the licence confers rights of occupation in a hostel.

Section 1(2) of the Protection from Eviction Act 1977 provides that a person commits a criminal offence if he unlawfully deprives or attempts to deprive a residential occupier of his occupation. (A residential occupier is broadly defined so that it includes tenants and licensees.)

This section spreads the net of criminal liability widely. For example, a landlord, or an agent, who attempts to evict a tenant (who is not an excluded tenant) without a court order will commit an offence. There is, however, within section 1(2) a defence: the person who evicts or attempts to evict a residential occupier will not incur criminal liability if he can prove that he believed, or had reasonable cause to believe, that the residential occupier had ceased to reside in the premises.

In order for actions to constitute a crime under section 1(2) they must have the character of an eviction. So, where an occupier is locked out of the premises on an isolated occasion for a limited period of time (such as overnight) normally no offence under section 1(2) is committed. (Nevertheless, the short-term deprivation of occupation which falls short of eviction may well constitute harassment.) In exceptional circumstances, however, the court may decide that short-term deprivation of occupation does amount to the crime of unlawful eviction. Such exceptional circumstances may arise if at the time of the exclusion of the occupier from the premises

o the landlord had the intention of excluding the occupier on a permanent basis and
o the occupier thought that he had been permanently excluded and
o the occupier was subsequently readmitted only because the landlord subsequently had a change of heart.

harassment

The Protection from Eviction Act 1977 (as amended by the Housing Act 1988) creates offences of harassment under section 1(3) and under section 1(3A). One fundamental requirement is common to both offences: it must be proved that the person accused was guilty of one of the following:

o persistently withholding services from the occupier
o persistently withdrawing services from the occupier
o performing acts likely to interfere with the peace or comfort of the occupier
o performing acts likely to interfere with the peace or comfort of members of the occupier's family.

Actions which would fall within the the scope of the offences of harassment would include cutting off the supply of gas and electricity to the premises occupied by a tenant, and undertaking repair work in such a way that the occupier could not reasonably be expected to remain in occupation.

In addition to proving that the acts of harassment were committed, it must be established that the accused had the necessary state of mind. In this respect the two offences of harassment differ. They also differ in that harassment under section 1(3) can be committed by anyone, while the offence created by section 1(3A) can only be committed by the landlord (or licensor) or by his agent.

harassment under section 1(3)
In relation to harassment under section 1(3) of the Protection from Eviction Act 1977, it must be shown that the person intended that the occupier would

○ give up occupation of the premises, or
○ refrain from exercising rights in respect of the premises, or
○ refrain from pursuing a remedy in respect of the premises.

harassment under section 1(3A)
For the new offence of harassment under section 1(3A) of the Protection from Eviction Act 1977 the state of mind required is less specific. What is required is that the accused knew, or had reasonable cause to believe, that the conduct was likely to cause the occupier either to give up occupation of the premises, or to refrain from exercising rights or pursuing a remedy in respect of the premises.

Section 1(3B) creates a defence by providing that the landlord does not commit an offence if he proves that he had reasonable cause for undertaking the particular acts in question.

using or threatening violence in order to get into premises
In addition to the offences created by the Protection from Eviction Act 1977, the law has also established criminal liability under the Criminal Law Act 1977 for using or threatening violence in order to gain entry to premises. Even in situations involving an excluded tenancy or an excluded licence, a landlord who wishes to recover possession of the premises must be careful not to fall foul of the Criminal Law Act 1977.

Section 6 provides that any person who 'without lawful authority' uses or threatens to use violence to secure entry to premises commits an offence. Where a tenancy or licence has come to an end, the fact that the landlord has a legal right to recover possession does not mean that he has 'lawful authority' for the purposes of this provision. For the offence to be committed, in addition to there being violence or the threat of violence, there must be someone on the premises at the time at which entry is sought, and that person must oppose the entry; also, the person using the violence must know that there is someone on the premises.

The offences created by the 1977 Act present certain problems for landlords. For example, what should the landlord do if an excluded tenant, whose tenancy has come to an end, refuses to vacate the premises? The landlord may lawfully recover possession by peaceable means. However, there is always a danger that such an attempt to recover possession will lead to violence. The better course of action for the landlord is to bring legal proceedings to obtain an order for possession from the court. (This can be achieved quickly and cheaply by way of summary proceedings in the county court.)

civil liability and criminal acts

The Housing Act 1988 has brought about a change in the law by providing that in certain circumstances, if criminal liability has been established under section 1 of the Protection from Eviction Act 1977, the conviction can be used as evidence in civil proceedings under the Housing Act 1988.

A number of conditions must be satisfied before civil liability under section 27 of the Housing Act 1988 can be established:

○ the acts in question must have taken place after 9 June 1988
○ the acts in question must have been committed by the landlord or an agent of the landlord
○ the occupier must have given up his occupation of the premises as a consequence of acts which would amount to unlawful eviction under section 1(2) or harassment under section 1(3A) of the Protection from Eviction Act 1977.

If these conditions are satisfied, the landlord is liable to pay damages to the former occupier. Damages for unlawful eviction are to be computed under section 28, which provides, in general terms, that the former occupier is entitled by way of damages to the difference in value between

○ the value of the premises with the occupier in occupation and the value of the premises on the assumption that the occupier no longer has a right of occupation.

Where the former occupier was a tenant with security of tenure under either the Rent Act 1977 or the Housing Act 1988, it is likely that damages will be substantial. However, if the occupation of the former occupier was in any event precarious (which will be the case where the former occupier was a periodic licensee or an assured shorthold tenant) damages will presumably be much lower.

There are a number of qualifications to the position described above:

○ if the former occupier is reinstated, no liability under section 27 arises

○ the court may reduce the amount of damages to be awarded to the former occupier if he has not acted reasonably

○ the landlord can escape liability if it is established that he reasonably believed that the occupier had ceased to occupy the premises, or if he reasonably believed that he had reasonable grounds for acting in the way he did.

The fact that the landlord is liable under section 27 does not preclude a tenant from pursuing other civil remedies against the landlord (although damages can be recovered only once in respect of any particular loss). Where there is no remedy under the 1988 Act the occupier may pursue various remedies under the common law.

the covenant for quiet enjoyment

At common law, a landlord's liability for evicting or harassing the tenant may be based on a breach of the landlord's implied obligation not to disturb the tenant's occupation. If the lease does not contain the relevant express provision, the law will imply into the lease what in legal language is called a 'covenant for quiet enjoyment'. This covenant imposes on the landlord an obligation to allow the tenant to use the premises peacefully and to exercise all his rights as a tenant.

The landlord will be in breach of this obligation if he does acts which physically interfere with the tenant's use and occupation of the premises. The following actions by the landlord will amount to a breach of covenant:

○ removing the tenant's belongings from the premises while the tenant is out
○ changing the locks and refusing to allow the tenant back in
○ cutting off services (gas, water, electricity) to the premises occupied by the tenant
○ removing the doors and windows of the premises
○ erecting scaffolding in such a way that the tenant's access is obstructed.

Where an occupier is a licensee, there can be no implied covenant of quiet enjoyment as such (since covenants characterise a lease and not a licence). However, the courts may imply terms into a contractual licence. For example, where the licensor acts in such a way that the licensee is effectively prevented from using the premises as envisaged when the parties entered into the licence agreement, the licensee should be able to establish that the licensor is in breach of his implied contractual obligations.

liability in tort

Tort is a category of law dealing with wrongful behaviour which causes a loss or damage to someone who may then seek redress through the civil courts.

In addition to contractual liability, a landlord (or licensor) may be liable in tort. Section 27 of the Housing Act 1988 creates a liability in tort for unlawful eviction. There are many other bases of liability in tort, of which a number may be relevant in the context of housing disputes.

Where premises are occupied by a tenant (but not by a licensee) a landlord who enters the premises either without authority under the lease or without the permission of the tenant commits the tort of trespass to land. A tort is also committed by a landlord or licensor who perpetrates physical violence against the occupier, or who intentionally damages the occupier's property. A landlord or licensor may also be liable to an occupier for the tort of nuisance if he performs acts which interfere with the occupier's reasonable enjoyment of the property. Many acts of harassment (such as cutting off services, or playing loud music late at night) will amount to the tort of nuisance.

what the occupier can do about it

In general terms, an occupier who has been evicted, or subjected to harassment, will be looking for two different types of remedy – an injunction and/or damages.

injunctions

In many cases, the most relevant remedy for an occupier will be an injunction. An injunction is an order from the court requiring a person to do or refrain from doing something.

In cases of eviction, the court may grant an injunction requiring the landlord to allow the tenant back into occupation. (An order in this form will prevent the tenant from recovering damages under section 27 of the Housing Act 1988.) In cases of harassment, an injunction can be made ordering the landlord to stop further harassment.

A person who fails to comply with the terms of an injunction commits a contempt of court. Penalties for contempt of court include fines and, in extreme cases, imprisonment.

damages

In certain cases, an injunction may be a sufficient remedy. However, there are few situations in which financial compensation will not be appropriate. If an evicted tenant does not wish to be reinstated to the premises, the only available form of redress is damages. Even where an injunction is obtained, the occupier will often have suffered financial loss (such as damage to property, or the cost of alternative accommodation) for which damages can be sought. As long as the occupier can establish that the defendant (landlord, or landlord's agent, for example, or a neighbour) has committed a civil wrong (a breach of contract, a breach of covenant or a tort) he will be entitled to damages. The court will make the appropriate decision.

An occupier who has suffered financial loss as a result of a civil wrong committed by the landlord (or licensor) may recover special damages, general damages and, in certain instances, exemplary damages.

special damages and general damages
Under special damages, the occupier may recover the actual, quantifiable out-of-pocket expenses. So, if as a result of unlawful eviction, a tenant has had to stay in a hotel for three nights pending reinstatement, these costs (if reasonable) can be recovered as special damages.

The occupier may recover general damages for more intangible losses, such as distress, pain and suffering and inconvenience.

when exemplary damages may be awarded
Exemplary damages may be awarded in a serious case of unlawful eviction. Exemplary damages are not awarded for breach of contract, but in any case in which exemplary damage might be at issue, it should be possible to frame the occupier's action against the landlord or licensor in terms of tort. The

principle on which exemplary damages are awarded was defined by Lord Devlin (in *Rookes v Barnard,* a case decided in 1964) in the following terms:

"Where a defendant with a cynical disregard for the plaintiff's rights has calculated that the money to be made out of his wrongdoing will probably exceed the damages at risk, it is necessary for the law to show that it cannot be broken with impunity. This category is not confined to moneymaking in the strict sense. It extends to cases in which the defendant is seeking to gain at the expense of the plaintiff some object - perhaps some property which he covets – which either he could not obtain at all or not obtain except at a price greater than he wants to put down. Exemplary damages can properly be awarded whenever it is necessary to teach a wrongdoer that tort does not pay."

It seems that in order to recover exemplary damages it is not necessary for the occupier to prove that the landlord did actually make a profit, since exemplary damages are not limited to cases where the landlord has been successful in evicting the tenant. (In cases of unlawful eviction, exemplary damages may exceed £1,000.)

warning

In general terms, these remedies outlined above can only be pursued through the legal process. Civil litigation is, however, both complex and slow. A tenant who wishes to take action against the landlord as a result of eviction or harassment should seek professional legal advice.

GLOSSARY

assignment
sale or transfer of the whole of a tenant's interest in a lease to another person

common law
the traditional law of England and Wales, derived from custom and judges' intepretation (as against statute law)

contract
a legally binding agreement; can be oral, but where it concerns land it should be in writing

covenant
an undertaking between landlord and tenant whereby they are bound to do certain things, such as to pay the rent or to repair; may be express (that is, set out in the lease) or implied

county court
court which deals with small civil cases, including disputes between landlord and tenant (generally, the amount at stake must not be more than £5,000)

criminal law
the part of the law which punishes behaviour harmful to the community as a whole, as against the civil law which confers rights and duties on individual people

curtilage
piece of ground (such as a courtyard) or part of a building near to and belonging to a house

deemed occupation
where the non-tenant spouse's occupation of a dwelling is treated as if it were the tenant's occupation, for the purposes of

satisfying the 'occupation' requirement under the statutory schemes of protection (for example an assured tenancy)

determination
when an interest in land comes to an end or ceases

disposition
any transferring of an interest in land, for example a sale, a gift, a lease, or by will

enfrancisement
tenant with long lease buying the freehold of the property under the Leasehold Reform Act 1967

equitable interest
rights in a property which fall short of legal title, for example where a lease is not properly created it may be an equitable lease

estate
person's interest in land (may be freehold or leasehold)

excluded tenancies
lettings in which the tenant does not enjoy statutory protection from eviction.

exclusive possession
the right to keep all others out of premises, including the landlord

forfeiture
the means by which a landlord can bring a lease to an early end following a breach of covenant by the tenant

freehold
absolute ownership of real property, which will continue with no limitation of time (as against leasehold)

grant
formal giving or transferring

ground rent
small sum payable periodically to the landlord (the ground owner) by tenant who holds leasehold property on a long lease

High Court
the principal court which deals with civil cases in England and Wales; there is no restriction as to the amount at stake

Housing Corporation
the supervisory body of non-profit making housing associations; also responsible for approval of organisations that have the right to acquire housing from local authorities or other public sector landlords under Part IV of the Housing Act 1988

interest in land
a right to, stake in, or any form of ownership of, property such as a house or flat

joint tenants
two (or more) people who hold property jointly in such a way that when one dies the whole property automatically passes to the survivor

Land Charges Department
a government department in Plymouth where rights over, and interests in, unregistered property are recorded; charges are registered against the name of the owner, not the property concerned

landlord
the owner of property who grants a lease or sub-lease of the property; the word is interchangeable with lessor

Land Registry
a government department where details of, and rights in, properties with a registered title are recorded

lease
written contact of letting; if for more than 3 years, it must be by deed to be legal

leasehold
ownership of property for a certain period under a lease which sets out the rights and duties of the leaseholder and the landlord (as against freehold)

legal charge
mortgage

licence
the right to use premises, as a personal privilege, without acquiring an interest in the property

offence
a breach of the criminal law

periodic tenancy
a tenancy for a short but definite period (for example, one month) which continues for such further periods until ended by notice

possesson action
exercising the powers or controls of ownership; procedure whereby a landlord goes to the court to evict a tenant or other lawful residential occupier

real property
land and any building on it

re-entry
lawfully retaking possession of a property

registered land
when the title or ownership of freehold or leasehold property has been registered at the Land Registry and its ownership is guaranteed by the state

relief
redress or remedial action; for example where the tenant's lease is allowed by the court to continue despite the fact that the landlord has obtained a judgment for forfeiture

remedy
legal redress

residential occupier
someone who lives in the property as his home

reversion
an interest in property which will eventually return to the original owner (or his successors) when the time during which another person holds the property comes to an end

section
a subdivision of a statute, always numbered and in many cases divided into sub-sections

secure tenant
an individual who occupies as his only or principal home a property of which the landlord is a local authority, or a county council, or a housing association or one of a few other public sector landlords

security of tenure
the right to remain in possession

statute
an act of parliament

statute law
body of law enacted in acts of parliament and their subordinate legislation (as against common law)

statutory instrument
document which makes or confirms legislation that is subordinate to an act of parliament, such as rules, regulations, orders

sub-lease
a lease carved out of another lease, necessarily for a shorter period, created by a person who has only a leasehold interest in the property

sub-tenant
tenant who leases property from a landlord who owns a leasehold, not a freehold interest in that property. It is possible for a chain of tenancies to be built up running from the freeholder (the head-landlord) to his tenant and down to a sub-tenant, then to a sub-sub-tenant and so on. Each tenant becomes the landlord of his own sub-tenant down to the last link in the chain – the tenant in actual occupation

superior landlord
someone with a higher interest than the tenant's immediate landlord; if Mr A, a freeholder, grants a 99 year lease to Mrs B, and Mrs B then grants a 21 year lease to Mr C, Mr A is the superior landlord

tenant
the person to whom a lease is granted; the word is interchangeable with lessor

title
ownership of a property

transfer
a formal deed which passes the freehold ownership of registered land from the seller to the buyer; where the land is unregistered, there is a conveyance (not a transfer)

unregistered land
property – freehold or leasehold – the title or ownership of which has not been registered at the Land Registry, so that the buyer must investigate the validity of the seller's title to it.

INDEX

Other Consumer Publications

Getting work done on your house

is a practical guide to successfully having work done on your house from renewing gutters to building an extension. It will help you to minimise the risk of frustration and disappointment sometimes experienced when trying to explain to a professional just what you want done. The whole process, from deciding what job needs to be done to final payment is covered in detail.

It includes hiring a professional or doing it yourself, documents and regulations, specialist treatments and trade associations, and emergency repair work.

Which? way to buy, sell and move house

Whatever you are moving from or to, this book is an invaluable guide to what is involved.

It clarifies issues that have to be decided initially, such as location (town v country), type of property (house v flat), size and style. The expenses likely to arise are set out, from statutory fees to thank-you presents for helpers, with basic information about getting a mortgage.

There is advice on 'house-hunting' generally, with a detailed section on what to look out for when viewing a flat – discussing the advantages and disadvantages of which floor, layout, heating, outgoings, garaging.

The book goes carefully through the procedure of making an offer, having a valuation and/or survey (including of a flat), conveyancing, exchange of contracts, completion. Problem areas are pointed out: the 'chain' of buyers and sellers, bridging loans, insurance, fixtures and fittings (to buy or not to buy).

Many practical matters have to be dealt with between contract and completion and there is a comprehensive section

on what has to be done at this interim stage (eg getting gas/
electricity, telephone services organised), including a helpful
checklist for change of address notifications.

Once the date of the move has been fixed, the arrangements
for the actual removal can be made – by a professional firm or
by doing it yourself with a hired van. The various factors to
consider with either method are discussed, such as cost,
insurance, personal wear and tear. A timetable for the moving
operation guides you to what will need to be done at different
stages, and there are useful hints on the practicalities of
packing, disposing of unwanted possessions, organising the
household (pets to kennels, children to friends). Activities on
the traumatic day of the move are itemised, and what will still
have to be done afterwards.

As a mirror image, the process of selling your property is
also dealt with. And there are sections on buying and selling in
Scotland.

As well as a wealth of factual information, the book is
enlivened by direct quotes from people who have recently
gone through the process of moving, with comments and hints
based on their experiences.

Earning money at home

explains how to brush up a skill or hobby into a money-making
venture. It gives advice on organising your family and dom-
estic life, on advertising your activities, costing and selling
your work, dealing with customers. There is information on
statutory and financial requirements for insurance, tax, ac-
counts, VAT, employing others. The book suggests way in
which your experience from a previous job could be utilised, or
a skill or hobby developed to a professional standard, or how
unexploited energy and ability can be used profitably.
Suggestions are made for improving your skills to a higher
standard, and the names and addresses are given of organisations that might be helpful.

Starting your own business

is the definitive guide for any budding entrepreneur with courage and imagination. It advises on defining precisely what product or skill you have to offer, how to raise the necessary capital and how to cope with the legal requirements to get you on the right road to realising your dream.

Throughout the book there are sources of advice and information to help the small businessman make a success of going it alone.

Understanding stress

Stress is inherent in the human condition and our century has intensified many stresses and added new ones, many of them psychological or social in nature. Some stresses are related to, or follow on, a specific identifiable event in the person's life: death, divorce, imprisonment rank high on the list. This book deals with stress and life events, stress from the world around us, at work, in the family. It explains the bodily reactions to stress and how to recognise the warning signs and how to help oneself cope with stress.

Divorce – legal procedures and financial facts

This book has been brought up to date to incorporate the great amount of new legislation which will affect people facing divorce today. It explains the procedure for an undefended divorce and deals with the financial facts to be faced when a marriage ends in divorce.

Aspects covered include getting legal advice, conciliation, legal aid and its drawbacks, the various financial and property orders the court can make, what can happen to the matrimonial home, how to calculate needs and resources and face up to shortage of money after a divorce.

Throughout, it explains the laws relating to children and how to minimise the effects of their parents' divorce.

Wills and probate

There are still too many people who have not made their will. This book will help them to do so, not blindly but aware of all the tax implications, the consequences of divorce, the right choice of executors, the proper signing and witnessing of the will so that their wishes can be carried out simply and sensibly.

The second part of the book describes what has to be done, administratively, by the executors of the estate of someone who has died. The probate registry provides special machinery to deal with laymen who wish to do so without having a solicitor. This book supplements this by explaining, in detail, not only the probate registry procedure but all that goes before and what comes after. It highlights recent relevant changes in tax law and procedure.

The book explains the law and procedure in England and Wales and briefly explains the main differences which apply in Scotland.

What to do when someone dies

is a companion volume to *Wills and probate*. It aims to help those who have never had to deal with the arrangements that must be made after a death – getting a doctor's certificate and registering the death, deciding whether to bury or cremate, choosing an undertaker and a coffin, putting notices in the papers, selecting the form of service, claiming national insurance benefits. It explains the function of people with whom they will come in contact, often for the first time. They will get help and guidance from the doctor, the registrar, the undertaker, the clergyman, the cemetery or crematorium officials, the Department of Health and Social Security and, in some circumstances, the police and the coroner. However, it is the executor or nearest relative who has to make the decisions, often at a time of personal distress. The book describes what needs to be done, when, and how to set about it.

No attempt is made to deal with the personal or social aspects of death, such as the psychology of grief and shock, the rituals and conventions of mourning, or attitudes to death.

Buying, owning and selling a flat

Buying a flat is similar to buying a house in some respects, in others the procedure has elements of renting. Now that more and more people are becoming flat-buyers and flat-owners, this new book gathers together and explains in simple terms all those areas of the law that are of particular concern to actual and potential flat-owners.

The book describes the different types of leasehole, outlines conveyancing procedure, tells the layman how to read a lease and what to look out for; explains ground rent and service charges, covenants, maintenance; examines the important relationship with the landlord and with neighbours.

The advantages and disadvantages of buying a flat jointly with someone else are discussed, and what happens when you want to sell.

The book explains the law and procedure in England and Wales and briefly explains the system which applies in Scotland.

Understanding cancer

explains the nature and causes of the disease most people find more frightening than any other. It tells you how to recognise some of the symptoms and avoid some of the risks, and explains how cancer is diagnosed. It goes into the details of various forms of treatment: surgery, radiotherapy, chemotherapy, including their possible side effects, and takes an objective look at the role of alternative/complementary therapies. It describes some of the advances in cancer research but does not pretend that these will soon provide the long awaited cure. The book deals with advanced cancer and terminal care but stresses that cancer must not be regarded as inevitably fatal.

Consumer Publications are available from Consumers' Association, Castlemead, Gascoyne Way, Hertford SG14 1LH, and from booksellers.